P9-CEJ-277

T 35476   932 STR

Life in ancient Egypt
Author: Streissguth, Thomas.
Reading Level: 9.6 Upper Grades
Point Value: 6.0
ACCELERATED READER QUIZ quiz: 51614

Wheeasset Middle School
Library

THE WAY
PEOPLE
LIVE

Life in Ancient Egypt

Titles in The Way People Live series include:

Cowboys in the Old West
Games of Ancient Rome
Life Among the Great Plains
  Indians
Life Among the Ibo Women of
  Nigeria
Life Among the Indian Fighters
Life Among the Pirates
Life Among the Samurai
Life Among the Vikings
Life During the Black Death
Life During the Crusades
Life During the French
  Revolution
Life During the Gold Rush
Life During the Great
  Depression
Life During the Middle Ages
Life During the Renaissance
Life During the Russian
  Revolution
Life During the Spanish
  Inquisition
Life in a Japanese American
  Internment Camp
Life in a Medieval Castle
Life in a Medieval Monastery
Life in a Nazi Concentration
  Camp
Life in Ancient Athens
Life in Ancient China
Life in Ancient Greece
Life in Ancient Rome

Life in a Wild West Show
Life in Charles Dickens's
  England
Life in the Amazon Rain Forest
Life in the American Colonies
Life in Communist Russia
Life in the Elizabethan Theater
Life in Genghis Khan's Mongolia
Life in the Hitler Youth
Life in Moscow
Life in the North During the
  Civil War
Life in the South During the
  Civil War
Life in Tokyo
Life in the Warsaw Ghetto
Life in War-Torn Bosnia
Life of a Medieval Knight
Life of a Nazi Soldier
Life of a Roman Slave
Life of a Roman Soldier
Life of a Slave on a Southern
  Plantation
Life on Alcatraz
Life on a Medieval Pilgrimage
Life on an African Slave Ship
Life on an Everest Expedition
Life on Ellis Island
Life on the American Frontier
Life on the Oregon Trail
Life on the Underground
  Railroad
Life Under the Jim Crow Laws

THE WAY
PEOPLE
LIVE

Life in Ancient Egypt

by Thomas Streissguth

Lucent Books, P.O. Box 289011, San Diego, CA 92198-9011

On Cover: Ancient Egyptian fresco
depicting people harvesting crops.

Library of Congress Cataloging-in-Publication Data

Streissguth, Thomas, 1958–
    Life in ancient Egypt / by Thomas Streissguth.
        p. cm. — (The way people live)
Includes bibliographical references (p.) and index.
    Summary: Discusses life in ancient Egypt including: work, the Pharaoh and
his court, Egyptian art and artisans, preparing for death, and leisure time.
    ISBN 1-56006-643-1 (hard cover : alk. paper)
    1. Egypt—Civilization—To 332 B.C.—Juvenile literature. 2. Egypt—Social
life and customs—To 332 B.C.—Juvenile literature. [1. Egypt—Civilization—
To 332 B.C. 2. Egypt—Social life and customs—To 332 B.C.] I. Title. II.
Series.
    DT61.S888 2001
    932—dc21
                                                                00-010261

Copyright 2001 by Lucent Books, Inc., P.O. Box 289011, San Diego, California,
92198-9011

No part of this book may be reproduced or used in any other form or by any
other means, electrical, mechanical, or otherwise, including, but not limited to,
photocopy, recording, or any information storage and retrieval system, without
prior written permission from the publisher.

Printed in the U.S.A.

Contents

Discovering the Humanity in Us All

Books in The Way People Live series focus on groups of people in a wide variety of circumstances, settings, and time periods. Some books focus on different cultural groups, others, on people in a particular historical time period, while others cover people involved in a specific event. Each book emphasizes the daily routines, personal and historical struggles, and achievements of people from all walks of life.

To really understand any culture, it is necessary to strip the mind of the common notions we hold about groups of people. These stereotypes are the archenemies of learning. It does not even matter whether the stereotypes are positive or negative; they are confining and tight. Removing them is a challenge that's not easily met, as anyone who has ever tried it will admit. Ideas that do not fit into the templates we create are unwelcome visitors—ones we would prefer remain quietly in a corner or forgotten room.

The cowboy of the Old West is a good example of such confining roles. The cowboy was courageous, yet soft-spoken. His time (it is always a he, in our template) was spent alternatively saving a rancher's daughter from certain death on a runaway stagecoach, or shooting it out with rustlers. At times, of course, he was likely to get a little crazy in town after a trail drive, but for the most part, he was the epitome of inner strength. It is disconcerting to find out that the cowboy is human, even a bit childish. Can it really be true that cowboys would line up to help the cook on the trail drive grind coffee, just hoping he would give them a little stick of peppermint candy that came with the coffee shipment? The idea of tough cowboys vying with one another to help "Coosie" (as they called their cooks) for a bit of candy seems silly and out of place.

So is the vision of Eskimos playing video games and watching MTV, living in prefab housing in the Arctic. It just does not fit with what "Eskimo" means. We are far more comfortable with snow igloos and whale blubber, harpoons and kayaks.

Although the cultures dealt with in Lucent's The Way People Live series are often historically and socially well known, the emphasis is on the personal aspects of life. Groups of people, while unquestionably affected by their politics and their governmental structures, are more than those institutions. How do people in a particular time and place educate their children? What do they eat? And how do they build their houses? What kinds of work do they do? What kinds of games do they enjoy? The answers to these questions bring these cultures to life. People's lives are revealed in the particulars and only by knowing the particulars can we understand these cultures' will to survive and their moments of weakness and greatness.

This is not to say that understanding politics does not help to understand a culture. There is no question that the Warsaw ghetto, for example, was a culture that was brought about by the politics and social ideas of Adolf

Hitler and the Third Reich. But the Jews who were crowded together in the ghetto cannot be understood by the Reich's politics. Their life was a day-to-day battle for existence, and the creativity and methods they used to prolong their lives is a vital story of human perseverance that would be denied by focusing only on the institutions of Hitler's Germany. Knowing that children as young as five or six outwitted Nazi guards on a daily basis, that Jewish policemen helped the Germans control the ghetto, that children attended secret schools in the ghetto and even earned diplomas—these are the things that reveal the fabric of life, that can inspire, intrigue, and amaze.

Books in The Way People Live series allow both the casual reader and the student to see humans as victims, heroes, and onlookers. And although humans act in ways that can fill us with feelings of sorrow and revulsion, it is important to remember that "hero," "predator," and "victim" are dangerous terms. Heaping undue pity or praise on people reduces them to objects, and strips them of their humanity.

Seeing the Jews of Warsaw only as victims is to deny their humanity. Seeing them only as they appear in surviving photos, staring at the camera with infinite sadness, is limiting, both to them and to those who want to understand them. To an object of pity, the only appropriate response becomes "Those poor creatures!" and that reduces both the quality of their struggle and the depth of their despair. No one is served by such two-dimensional views of people and their cultures.

With this in mind, The Way People Live series strives to flesh out the traditional, two-dimensional views of people in various cultures and historical circumstances. Using a wide variety of primary quotations—the words not only of the politicians and government leaders, but of the real people whose lives are being examined—each book in the series attempts to show an honest and complete picture of a culture removed from our own by time or space.

By examining cultures in this way, the reader will notice not only the glaring differences from his or her own culture, but also will be struck by the similarities. For indeed, people share common needs—warmth, good company, stability, and affirmation from others. Ultimately, seeing how people really live, or have lived, can only enrich our understanding of ourselves.

The Story of Ancient Egypt

The ancient kingdom of Egypt lay along the fertile valley of the Nile River in northeastern Africa. For nearly three millennia, the Egyptian pharaohs (kings) ruled one of the ancient world's richest and most powerful nations. So long was Egypt's history that modern writers measure its time not in years but in dynasties: clans that ruled the country for decades and, in some cases, for more than a century. The history of ancient Egypt includes thirty-one dynasties and the reigns of hundreds of monarchs, as well as a "predynastic" period of Egyptian civilization that began thousands of years before the first king unified the country.

The Unification of Egypt and the Old Kingdom

According to legend, a ruler named Menes was the first to unite the rival lands of Lower (northern) and Upper (southern) Egypt, an event that historians date to around 3100 B.C. Menes established the First Dynasty, and this event marks the beginning of the ancient Egyptian kingdom. At about the same time as the unification of Egypt came important advances in agriculture, metalworking, transportation, and communication in the Nile valley and in the Delta region (where the Nile fans out into several branches before reaching the Mediterranean Sea). During this time, the Egyptians also invented a system of hieroglyphs, or picture symbols.

Menes and the other kings of the First Dynasty ruled during a period of Egyptian history known as the Old Kingdom. At this time, the city of Memphis, just south of the Nile Delta, served as the capital of ancient Egypt. As Egypt's population increased, the kings ruling from Memphis set about conquering neighboring lands, and as a result the realm grew wealthier. Menes' successor, a king named Aha, invaded Nubia, the land lying south of Egypt. Another First Dynasty king, Den, successfully fought the Bedouin, a nomadic people who lived in the deserts lying both east and west of the Nile valley.

The Old Kingdom ended with the Eighth Dynasty, about 2150 B.C. At this time, Egyptian nobles were raising their own armies, building their own temples, and ruling cities and nomes (provinces) from their own palaces. But Egypt fell into disunion; its people suffered as civil war wracked the country. At the same time, the climate grew drier, forcing villagers to move closer to the Nile in order to irrigate their fields. From time to time, the annual summer flood of the Nile failed, bringing drought, crop failures, and starvation.

The Rise of Thebes

This time of chaos, known to historians as the First Intermediate Period, ended when Mentuhotep I ascended the Egyptian throne and defeated the rebellious nobles. Mentuhotep

This alabaster and ivory perfume vessel, created ca. 1347–1337 B.C., symbolizes the legendary unification of Lower and Upper Egypt under a single ruler around 3100 B.C.

reunited the country and established a new capital in his home city of Thebes, which lay about two hundred miles south (upriver) of Memphis. Mentuhotep's Eleventh Dynasty reign marked the beginning of the Middle Kingdom.

The Middle Kingdom proved to be a prosperous time. The Twelfth Dynasty, which began around 1938 B.C., represented a golden age for the ancient Egyptians. The eight kings of the Twelfth Dynasty enjoyed long reigns, averaging twenty-two years each, and orderly successions. The country remained at peace, while the fertile fields adjoining the Nile produced bumper harvests of grain. The abundant crops allowed Egypt to trade with foreign nations for goods it lacked, such as wood. The art of sculpture also flourished; artisans in the service of the royal court created magnificent busts and statues in marble, granite, and many other kinds of hard stone. Egypt's troublesome nobles were brought to the royal court in Thebes as a means of preventing rebellion and disorder in the provinces.

The Hyksos and the New Kingdom

The peace and prosperity of the Middle Kingdom did not last, however. At the end of the Twelfth Dynasty, a dynasty of foreign rulers, the Hyksos, arrived in Egypt. Historians believe the Hyksos may have come from Palestine, the land neighboring Egypt to the northeast. While the Hyksos kings reigned in the Delta region, a rival dynasty controlled the old capital of Thebes. Then, in the early sixteenth century B.C., one of these Theban kings, Seqenenre, campaigned against the Hyksos ruler Apopi. Seqenenre was killed in battle, but his son Kamose drove the Hyksos out of Egypt. In 1567 B.C., Ahmose, the brother of Kamose, claimed the throne of the reunified nation and established the Eighteenth Dynasty.

The Eighteenth Dynasty began Egypt's New Kingdom. Ahmose's successors established a large standing army and built a string of fortresses along the Nile River in Upper Egypt. These outposts extended the kingdom south and protected Egypt's trading caravans from the raids of desert peoples. The outposts served their purpose well: Egypt grew rich by trade with Arabia and with Nubia, the land to the south, where traders brought gold, ivory, ebony, slaves, ostrich feathers, and leopard skins from central Africa to exchange for Egyptian grain.

Egypt's power and prestige increased during the Nineteenth Dynasty, when Seti I

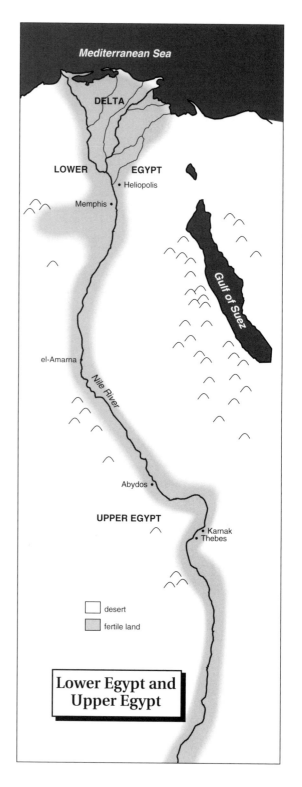

Lower Egypt and Upper Egypt

and his son Ramses II extended Egyptian influence to Syria and Asia Minor. Ramses made an important peace treaty with the Hittite Empire, in Asia Minor, and through princes allied to his government, he also controlled most of Palestine and Syria. To celebrate his many military and diplomatic achievements, Ramses ordered the building of a great mortuary temple, the Ramesseum, where granite statues and towering obelisks were raised in his honor. Ramses also had a small army of stonecutters and sculptors carve depictions of his royal family into a mountainside at Abu Simbel, in Upper Egypt.

Under Seti and Ramses, Egypt reached the height of its geographic reach and military power. But after Ramses' death, Egypt faced a new enemy: the "Sea Peoples" who came from the lands bordering the Mediterranean Sea to the north. After the attack of the Sea Peoples, Egypt began a long decline. The Egyptians lost their faith in the traditional gods and in the divine nature of their kings. Foreigners—Asians from the east and Libyans from the west—settled in Egypt, taking command of the army and the government. By the time of the Twenty-second Dynasty, which began in 945 B.C., the sons of Libyans were ruling over Egypt.

The Egyptian realm continued its decline over the next six centuries. Nubians, Assyrians, and then Persians claimed the throne of Egypt, and for more than two hundred years Egypt remained a satrap, or province, that paid tribute to the emperors of Persia. In 332 B.C., the Macedonian king Alexander the Great defeated the Persians and incorporated Egypt into his expanding empire. After Alexander's death, the Macedonian Empire broke up, and the Macedonian general Ptolemy took control of Egypt.

Ptolemy founded a new dynasty, in which the rulers spoke Greek and brought Greek culture to their new capital at Alexandria, on the Mediterranean Sea. The Ptolemaic rulers dressed and appeared as pharaohs and built new shrines to the old Egyptian gods, but they lived as foreigners among the people they ruled. Finally, the last independent ruler of Egypt, the Ptolemaic queen Cleopatra, was defeated by the Roman ruler Octavius in 30 B.C. After Cleopatra committed suicide, Egypt became a province of Rome, and the ancient Egyptian state came to a dramatic end.

Life and Work Along the Nile River

The Nile flows northward through Egypt, gradually broadening as it passes the villages, fields, and distant red cliffs of the valley. As the river broadens into the Delta, smaller streams branch away from the main course and flow through tangled, dense growths of reeds. In ancient times, clumps of easily harvested papyrus grew here in abundance, providing Egyptian villagers with the raw material for baskets, rope, boats, tools, and bedding mats.

Wildlife was abundant in the Nile Delta. Plovers, pigeons, ibis, herons, cranes, ducks, and quail fed on insects and fish. Hippopotamuses shared the marshes with crocodiles, weasles, hares, and wild cats. Birds and mammals all watched carefully for the poisonous snakes that slithered through the long Delta grasses. In most places, the land was too waterlogged or overgrown for farming, and as a result human habitation was sparse compared to the fertile Nile valley upstream. Instead, the Nile Delta was something like a vast wild park that, in the imaginations of the ancient Egyptians, closely resembled the paradise to come after death.

The Flood of the Nile

Egypt's farmers were completely dependent on the flooding of the Nile River for their livelihood. Each year, and always at the same time, the waters of the Nile and the Delta began to rise. Fed by monsoon rains falling far to the south, on the highlands of Ethiopia and eastern Africa, the inundation began in the summer and gradually moved north. After several weeks, the flood reached the fields of Lower Egypt, the Delta, and finally the river's mouth at the Mediterranean Sea. The river reached its highest point in September, then slowly returned to its main channel, leaving behind a layer of fertile silt in which plants could thrive.

For the Egyptians, the flood was a time for a national celebration, for it was a sign that the gods responsible for this miracle were tangibly rewarding them for their faith and offerings. A Hymn to the Nile, written during the New Kingdom, rejoices at the return of the flood:

> Hail to you, oh Nile, spring from the ground, come to keep the land alive . . . who inundates the fields that Re has created to make all the animals live . . . who produces barley and makes wheat grow, that the temples might be in festival. If he is sluggish, noses suffocate, everyone is impoverished. . . . If he rises, the land is in exultation, and everyone is in joy.[1]

The ancient Egyptians saw the Nile as a blessing that represented Egypt's fertility and prosperity. But when the Nile flood failed, as it occasionally did, the Egyptians took it as a sign of disfavor from the gods. A low flood, or no flood at all, was the worst kind of natural disaster for a people who also experienced dust storms, occasional earthquakes, and locust invasions. These were temporary phenomena,

Working the Land

The hard labor many peasants were subject to during the time of the flood—a season that might have been spent in rest—demonstrated to ancient Egypt's farmers that they were little better than slaves, useful possessions of the king to be discarded when no longer productive. The kingdom's system of laws and landholding reinforced this view.

To the omnipotent Egyptian kings belonged all of the kingdom's land. There was no private ownership of fields, roads, canals, or uncultivated terrain. But by Egyptian law, the people who lived on or near a tract of land had to work that land, and each year had to turn over their produce to the state. Their reward came in the form of small rations of grain and beer, doled out from the government's granaries and warehouses. Peasants were closely watched by overseers and tax collectors and punished severely for any infraction of the rules, any slacking, any underpayment of their taxes. They could not leave the land to find better employment elsewhere, nor did they have rights in court to ask for a redress of their grievances or a hearing of their complaints.

however, whereas the failure of the flood meant a long period of dry, unproductive fields and, as a result, many hungry people. If the royal and provincial governments had grain stored for such an occasion, then the people would eat, although not so well. If the public storage rooms were empty, or if their food could not be distributed, then poverty, disease, starvation, and sometimes cannibalism resulted. During one such bad year, around 2000 B.C., a priest named Heqanakhte wrote this description of a famine-stricken Lower Egypt to his relatives in Thebes:

> I arrived here and collected as much food for you as possible. The Nile, is it not in fact very low? And the food we have collected is proportionate to the flood. . . . Here, one has begun to eat people. Nowhere is there someone to whom nourishment is given.[2]

A Fertile Silt

The river's silt was rich in phosphates that renewed the soil, where barley and wheat were grown to provide the Egyptian staples of bread and beer. A system of irrigation canals ran parallel to the river's course on both sides of the Nile. Villagers cut dikes and ditches running across the valley from these canals to bring the water to permanent basins, where it could be stored and used during the dry seasons.

The productivity of the Nile valley allowed the Egyptians to store surpluses to guard against famine in times when the flood was low and crops failed. The river was the key to the nation's prosperity and the secret to its stability and longevity. According to the poet Paibes, who lived in the thirteenth century B.C.,

> [Egypt is] full of good things and provisions every day. Its channels abound in fish and its lakes in birds. Its fields are green with herbage and its banks bear dates. Its tall granaries are overflowing with barley and wheat. Garlic, leeks, lettuces and fruits are there for sustenance and wine surpassing honey. . . . He who dwells there is happy, for there the humble are like the mighty elsewhere.[3]

Peasants

In a society like Egypt's, which was dependent on what its farmers could grow, the peasants made up the kingdom's largest social class. They worked the land, digging the canals and irrigation ditches that fed the fields with water and silt from the Nile. They sowed and harvested staple foods such as wheat and barley as well as vegetables, flax, and fruit (with much of the land planted with crops, there was little room for livestock herds).

Hard work, lasting all through the daylight hours, was the peasants' daily lot. Historian Lionel Casson describes conditions in the countryside:

> To make the most of the land, Egyptian farmers and field hands had to labor unceasingly. Often it took ingenuity as well as brawn to survive. Farmers used simple tools, but put them to many uses. One large-headed, short-handled implement served to dig and shore up irrigation ditches after the harvest—and then did duty as a hoe during the next planting. Reaping was done by hand with a sickle; the same implement also cut clover for cattle and rushes for making mats. Everyone had to pitch in. Women, though busy with their domestic chores, doubled as field hands. At the harvest everyone poured out into the fields to gather the crop and to celebrate the fact that famine had once more been staved off.[4]

Yet compared with farmers of other lands, Egyptian peasants could consider themselves lucky, since the arduous job of cultivating the land was largely unnecessary. The ancient Greek traveler and historian Herodotus noted during his journey to Egypt in the fifth century B.C.,

Making up the Egyptian kingdom's largest social class, peasants labored ceaselessly to grow the food the nation needed. This wall painting of oxen threshing wheat was discovered in a tomb from the Eighteenth Dynasty.

> As things are at present these people get their harvests with less labor than anyone else in the world, the rest of the Egyptians included; they have no need to work with plough or hoe, or to use any other of the ordinary methods of cultivating their land; they merely wait for the river of its own accord to flood their fields; then, when the water has receded, each farmer sows his plot, turns pigs into it to tread in the seed, and then waits for the harvest.[5]

The mild climate of Egypt also played an important role in helping farmers. Although the land was hot in summer, it was also dry, with few storms to interrupt their work. A laborer or farmer could usually find a cool spot in the shade of a tree or a small shelter. As

James Breasted writes in his book *A History of the Ancient Egyptians*,

> In climate Egypt is a veritable paradise. . . . The air of Egypt is essentially that of the deserts within which it lies, and such is its purity and dryness that even an excessive degree of heat occasions but slight discomfort, owing to the fact that the moisture of the body is dried up almost as fast as it is exhaled.[6]

During the annual flood, there was little work to do in the fields. The farmers used their free time to build and repair homes, to visit family and friends in nearby villages, to bring craft goods to public markets, to hunt in the desert, or to fish in the Nile. Family members attended to the tombs of their ancestors, making ritual offerings and ensuring that the graves and monuments to the deceased were secure from vandals and robbers. During the flood season—which also happened to fall in the hottest time of the year—the kings also recruited peasants to work on state projects: digging and reinforcing canals, quarrying stone in the desert, and building temples, pyramids, and other monuments.

Bringing in the Crop

Although Egyptian farmers had it better than their counterparts elsewhere, life was still hard. After the flood receded, the season of exhausting, daylong labor began as the fields were planted, the plants cared for, and the mature crops harvested. Entire families set out from their villages to the fields early in the morning, accompanied by any seasonal laborers hired by the landowner to ensure that the work was carried out in good time. Farming tools included pickaxes and wooden hoes to break up dry soil; a small wooden plow that

This fresco painting depicts an Egyptian peasant plowing the land to prepare it for planting.

could be pulled by men, oxen, or cattle to break uncultivated land; a sickle made with a cutting edge of flint; and rakes, pitchforks, hammers, and saws made of stone whose nature and use went back to prehistoric times.

During the sowing, women and children followed closely behind the plow to scatter the seed, while the farmers turned their sheep, goats, and pigs loose to trample the seeds down into the soil. Once the seed was planted, it had to be watered. Some fields could be irrigated by canals that led water from the Nile. To carry water to higher ground, farmers used a pair of clay water jars

Time and the Nile

The regular annual flooding of the Nile aided the ancient Egyptians in the invention of their calendar. The Egyptian year was divided into three seasons of four months each. *Akhet* was the season of flood, which was heralded by the return of Sirius (the "Dog Star") to the eastern sky around what we know as July 19. During the season of *peret*, the land emerged from beneath the river's waters as the flood receded. *Shemu* was the season of drought, when the river ran low and the harvested fields grew dry.

The ancient Egyptians divided each day into twenty-four hours: twelve hours of day and twelve hours of night. To keep track of time, the Egyptians used water clocks known as clepsydra. These were small clay jars that allowed water to slowly escape from a small opening at their base. The inside of the jar was marked with a scale of the hours, which corresponded to the level of the water inside.

Another type of ancient Egyptian clock is described by R. W. Sloley as cited in Glanville's *The Legacy of Ancient Egypt*.

"The hours of the day were very roughly determined by simple shadow clocks, evolved independently of the clepsydra. Shadow clocks are still in use in country districts, and to this day the 'servant gapeth after the shadow'. . . when it is nearing time to knock off work.

In the East, except in towns, there is still little need for mean solar time, and clocks and watches in Arabia are altered daily at sunset to agree with the time of sunset as shown by the almanack. The day begins at sunset."

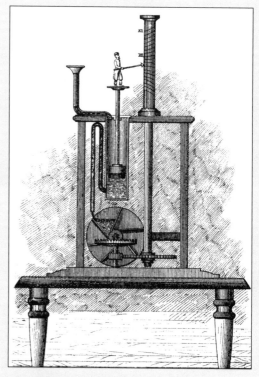

This illustration from 245 B.C. depicts a clepsydra, or water clock, which the Egyptians used to keep track of time.

suspended from a wooden board that was placed over their shoulders. This job was made easier around 1300 B.C., when the Egyptians began using the *shaduf*, a device for raising water from rivers and canals to higher levels. The *shaduf* was made up of a long pole that rested on a pivot. A water basket rested on one end of the pole, a counterweight on the other. The pole was dipped into the water source, then raised and swung to the higher ground, where the water was emptied from the basket into a ditch.

The *shemu*, or dry season, was the time of harvest. Grains were reaped with sickles, then collected into sheaves and brought away from the field. The harvesters piled donkeys and oxen high with the sheaves and then led them to threshing rooms, where the kernels of grain were separated from the stalks and the tough outer husks were removed. To do this, the crops were emptied out onto a stone floor and trampled by draft animals walking in endless circles. Women then took the grain outside for winnowing, tossing the grain into the air to be separated from the dry husks by the wind. Pierre Montet describes the threshing scene depicted in an Egyptian wall painting:

The floor of the threshing-floor is of beaten earth. When a sufficiently thick layer of grain has been spread, oxen are turned loose on it, accompanied by a number of men carrying whips and forks. While the oxen tread out the grain the men continually fork it over. The heat and the dust make this work very trying, but the oxdriver encourages his animals. . . . Every now and again an ox lowers his massive head and takes a mouthful of mixed grain and straw, but no one seems to mind.[7]

The farmer then brought the winnowed grain to the storehouses of his master, who was usually a member of the nobility. Scribes measured and recorded the harvest by weight, and workers poured the grain into tall, conical granaries. Local nobles, who oversaw the harvest as the king's representatives, collected all the produce of the land, paid their annual tributes to the king, supplied their own households, and then passed out the measure of rations to the peasants who had worked the land.

Besides grain, Egyptian farmers raised flax to be made into light and sheer linen. The stalks of the flax plant were twisted into balls, from which weavers could extract the fibers needed to make clothing. The Egyptians preferred plain white clothing, the better to keep their bodies cool and—for the better off—the best to show off any jewelry, amulets, or other adornments worn on special occasions. (So universal was the use of white clothing that wearing colored clothing marked one as a foreigner in ancient Egypt.)

Farmers also raised a wide variety of vegetables, including leeks, onions, lettuces, cucumbers, and beans. They cultivated these crops in smaller plots that could be irrigated by small channels dug from the river and the main canals year-round. Sesame and castor beans provided cooking oil, while jujube, fig, pomegranate, and date palm trees supplied fruits. Grapes were pressed into wine, the finest of which came from the Faiyum region, lying south of the Delta and west of the Nile valley. The Egyptians also collected honey from beehives made from dried mud. The honey-laden combs were taken from the beehives, then heated and strained, and the beeswax removed.

In addition to grain and vegetable crops, Egyptian farmers raised beef cattle, pigs, sheep, goats, and donkeys, which served as the principal beast of burden. Large herds were unknown, however, because forage and

This fresco, from a tomb in the Valley of the Kings, illustrates the preference of the ancient Egyptians for wearing white clothing.

pasture were limited. As a result, most peasant families considered meat a luxury. Beef and fowl could be preserved by drying in the sun and then storing in jars of salt. Milk, cheese, and butter were produced from the milk of cows. Geese, ducks, pigeons, and cranes were also raised on Egyptian farms.

The Homes of the People

Egyptian peasants lived in small, mud-brick homes. They made the bricks from clay that was placed in wooden forms, mixed with straw and cattle dung, and then dried in the sun. The houses were clustered together in small groups, often sharing common walls. Workmen living away from home lived in large barracks, in which a long series of small and simple rooms clustered around a dusty courtyard or a hallway that ran the length of the building.

For many families, home was only a single room, with reed mats covering dirt floors. Kitchens were outside or located in the corner of the single room. Cooking was done by the women of the household, who used small clay ovens to bake bread and cook vegetables and meat, when it was available. Because meat was scarce and therefore beyond the means of most peasants, fish was a much more common source of protein. Beer was a favored drink, served at all times of the day in homes, in palaces, and in public taverns. The beer was brewed from half-cooked barley loaves, which were mixed with the juice of dates in large vats. The liquid was strained and allowed to ferment, then poured into clay jars, which were tightly closed with a plaster stopper. The sealed jars allowed the beer to be transported without going stale or sour.

As a family's wealth increased, additional stories might be added to a home to provide sleeping quarters and storage space. The house facade was a solid wall broken only by the door and its frame. Windows with stone or wooden blinds to keep out dust and the sun were placed only on the second story, not on the ground floor. Often, a small open space or enclosed courtyard lay behind the house, on the side opposite the front of the home. The roof of the home provided further space for storing household goods and food.

Wealthier Egyptians provided themselves more spacious homes. As described by James Breasted,

> The houses of the rich were large and commodious. . . . The materials were wood and sun-dried brick, and the construction was light and airy as suited the climate. There were many latticed windows[;] on all sides the walls of the living rooms were largely a mere skeleton, like those of many Japanese houses. Against winds and sandstorms they could be closed by dropping gaily coloured hangings.[8]

These aristocratic homes had courtyard gardens, divided into square or rectangular plots lined with flowers and sometimes featuring a rectangular pool. In the courtyard the owner might plant date palms, sycamores, fig trees, pomegranates, acacias, tamarisk, and willow trees. Trees outside the front door shaded the entrance of the house.

Throughout the home the owners scattered natron, a chemical compound, or other special preparations to keep down pests such as rats, lizards, snakes, and insects. Stale rooms were fumigated with mixtures of resin and incense to give a pleasant smell. These preparations were imported and expensive, however, and most ordinary Egyptians could not afford them. Instead, they made do with constantly sweeping and airing their small one- or two-room homes, where the only furnishings might be a mat of reeds and a small stool, as well as the wooden headrests that Egyptians of all classes used as their pillows.

The Egyptians furnished their homes with simple furniture—chairs, beds, and stools—made from native Egyptian woods of acacia and sycamore. More prosperous Egyptian artisans could have afforded goods fashioned from cedar, cypress, pine, and other expensive woods imported from Syria and Lebanon. No matter how grand or humble, their homes shielded Egyptians from the noise and chaos of the dusty public streets and squares, where

Egyptian homes were generally made of brick and wood and contained simple furniture.

chickens, goats, and geese ran about, vying for scraps of food with household pets such as cats, dogs, and monkeys.

Family Life

At home, the men of ancient Egypt enjoyed the status of head of the household. Within the household, they were given deference by wives, children, and servants. Their word was considered the law within the house, and they held themselves responsible for the fortunes, or misfortunes, of the family.

Yet the women of Egypt enjoyed greater freedom and higher status than the women of any other ancient society. Several professions were open to them, such as temple dancers, mourners, musicians, and midwives. Women could manage estates, and a few worked as royal officials or administrators. Some were employed in workshops, and a very few may have worked as scribes. Women held an im-

portant religious status as priestesses; one woman of ancient Egypt even reached the rank of high priest of Amon-Re, one of the most powerful offices in the land. In contrast to women in many ancient societies, Egyptian women traveled freely outside their homes and wore clothing of their own choosing.

Women could own property in their own name; they could also inherit property such as land, livestock, household goods, and servants. They could freely enter into marriage agreements that set out in detail the property belonging to each partner in the marriage. After the marriage took place, Egyptian women had the right to one-third of the property accumulated by the couple as husband and wife. If the husband died, the widow was entitled to one-third of the community property, with the children receiving the remainder.

Women could adopt children of their own free will, divorce their husbands if they wished, and start a lawsuit without the help of a man. Like men, they could also turn themselves into

Women in Egypt enjoyed higher status and more freedom than women in other ancient societies. Among the professions open to them were temple dancer, musician, mourner, and midwife.

Egyptian law allowed women many rights: They could own property, adopt children, divorce their husbands while retaining one-third of the couple's goods, and dress and travel as they wished.

servants in another household, for the payment of a debt or as a form of security. Despite the freedom accorded women, as Barbara Mertz explains, they also were subject to harsh punishment for certain transgressions:

> There was one serious crime against marriage—infidelity. Since we have no Egyptian civil law codes, we have to infer from other sources just what constituted a crime, but several stories make it clear that adultery—for the wife, at least—was a dangerous game. There is one such story

about a great magician and his faithless wife. The lady must have been sorely tempted to take chances with a man of her husband's profession; of course, the seer found out. Her lover was given to a crocodile that, presumably, did something unpleasant to him. By the king's command, the wife was burned alive.[9]

Childhood and Marriage

For the first few years of their lives, children in ancient Egypt ran free under the watch of their parents, relatives, and, in wealthier households, servants. They amused themselves with board games and toys and used the village streets and squares as a common playground. The banks of the Nile provided many opportunities for adventure and exploration, but Egyptian parents warned their children against straying beyond the valley into the desert, the domain of dangerous animals, bandits, and hostile desert dwellers such as the Bedouin.

The universal mark of childhood in Egypt was the sidelock, a tuft of hair that was allowed to grow long from the side of the head while the rest of the hair was shaved off. When adolescence was reached and adult pursuits taken up, the sidelock was shorn off. At this time, life grew more serious—children became capable of helping their families in the fields or working as apprentices in their fathers' workshops.

Boys were encouraged to marry as soon as they could support themselves and a household. For young men, marriage marked the establishment of a domain of their own, within which wives were cherished as their most valuable and useful property. As suitors, the young men offered presents to the girl's family, and if accepted, both families arranged a marriage ceremony. Marriage contracts were then drawn up, in which the husband agreed to provide for the wife, and the wife agreed to bring certain possessions into the household (possessions that remained hers in the event of divorce). Once they were married, the young men moved out of their parents' homes to establish their own households.

An Old Kingdom wise man named Ptahotep had this advice for young men preparing for marriage:

> If you are a man of standing, you should establish your household and love your wife at home, as is proper. Fill her belly and clothe her back; ointment is the prescription for her body. Make her heart glad as long as you live—she is a profitable field for her lord. You should not contend with her at law; keep her from gaining control. . . . Let her heart be soothed through what may accrue to you; it means keeping her long in your house.

> When you are a young man and take yourself a wife and are settled in your house, remember how your mother gave birth to you, and all her raising of you besides. Do not let her blame you, so that she lifts her hands to god and he hears her lamentations. . . . Do not supervise your wife in her house if you know that she is capable; don't say to her, "Where is it? Get it for us!!" when she has [already] put it in the [most] useful place. Watch and be silent, so that you may recognize her talents.[10]

The most essential duty carried out by the son of any family was attending to the afterlife of his parents. When a mother or father died, the son arranged for the coffin, the place of burial, and the funeral rites; after the burial, he saw to the regular offerings of food and prayer and the recitation of prayers at the

The Disappearing Egyptian Buildings

Archaeologists hoping to uncover the structures that the people of ancient Egypt lived in usually come up empty-handed. Eventually, the wood, reeds, and mud brick of Egyptian homes crumbled away. A house lasted a few decades, at most, before its owners demolished it and replaced it with a new structure, using the abundant building materials provided by the Nile valley.

As a result of the practice of building atop older city sites, very little of most ancient Egyptian cities remains in the modern world, although some artifacts lie buried under rubble that has built up over millennia. Unfortunately, the Nile River's course has steadily shifted to the east over the centuries, flooding hundreds of ancient townsites and making excavation of these sites impossible. Even where flooding is not a problem, the mud brick of which Egyptian homes and palaces were made was plundered by builders in later times, so the buildings themselves cannot be excavated. The royal capital of Memphis, for example, largely disappeared during the Middle Ages, when builders dismantled its palaces and temples to build the Arabic capital of Cairo. In addition, for thousands of years, Egyptian farmers have quarried the crumbling mud brick from old and abandoned houses to use as a fertilizer known as *sebakh*. These practices left very little of the homes and public buildings where the ancient Egyptians carried on their everyday life.

The duty of arranging for a funeral ceremony for his parents was a crucial one for the son. This mural from ca. 1390–1336 B.C. depicts the transportation of funeral furniture.

tomb. If a parent died leaving only daughters behind, then this task fell to his or her brother.

A Secure Life

Even though day-to-day life involved hard labor, whether in planting and gathering crops or in building public monuments, the common people of Egypt saw some compensation in that life was secure from want and hunger. Historian Lionel Casson comments,

> The lot of the peasantry, though hard, was not without its compensations. An Egyptian peasant certainly knew more security

and had fewer worries than his counterpart in lands periodically laid waste by conquerors. It is true that his day was spent toiling in another man's fields. But the soil he served provided him and his family with sustenance, though it was usually frugal, and the river was liberal with its fish.[11]

Through most of its history, the isolated Egyptian nation did not suffer from foreign invasion. For the average laborer or peasant, the outside world was distant and strange; the center of the world, the true paradise on earth, was the valley of the Nile, where the people lived in peace thanks to the glory and the power of the kings who ruled over their land.

The Pharaoh and His Court

The social classes of ancient Egypt remained rigidly fixed, allowing very few to rise above the station in life to which they were born. Egyptian society imitated the pyramid: The largest number of people lived among the lowest classes of peasants and artisans while a single individual reigned at the apex, exercising absolute power as the king, a representative of the gods on earth. For the pharaoh, daily life was unlike that of any other Egyptian.

A Living Symbol of Egypt

In Egypt, kings were considered living embodiments of the nation and of the gods. In temple and tomb paintings, kings were depicted with the head of a falcon, a symbol of the god Horus, who according to myth was the first king of the land. The kings also possessed the power of magical utterance, in which they might summon divine powers by words alone. The ancient Egyptians believed that their king could use these powers to bring rain, find underground springs, defeat enemies on the battlefield, and ensure the annual flood of the Nile, a mysterious phenomenon that the Egyptians considered to be a magical event.

Through their personal power and authority, the kings held the nation together. The people of Egypt saw them as guardians of their safety, prosperity, and unity. For this reason, royal authority, especially during the Old Kingdom, was absolute. The deference

shown to the pharaoh knew no limits. According to historian Sir Alan Gardiner,

Evidently the power of the Pharaoh was paramount in every province of Old Kingdom life. The reverence shown to his person was abject in the extreme. One priestly attendant tells how by accident the king's scepter brushed against his foot and how great was his relief when his master refrained from striking him. Other high officers of state boast that they were permitted to kiss their sovereign's foot instead of the ground in front of him.[12]

According to Egyptian belief, the coronation of a new pharaoh took place in the heavens, in a ceremony carried out by the gods themselves. Coronation was also, of course, an earthly event carried out by human courtiers and officials. The coronation ceremony, also known as *kha*, always took place at the start of the Egyptian year, about July 19 in the modern calendar. At this time the waters of the Nile began to rise, an event that promised a good harvest as the year continued.

After the coronation took place, the king's divine status brought heavy responsibilities, as described by John A. Wilson in *The Culture of Ancient Egypt:*

There was no written and detailed statecraft for Egypt; there needed to be none where the state was summed up in the person of a god. . . . His alone was the au-

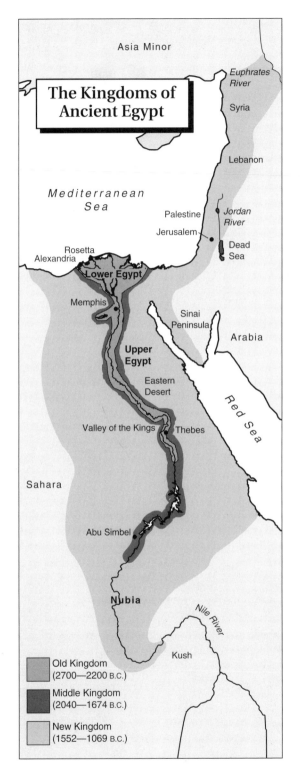

The Kingdoms of Ancient Egypt

Asia Minor

Euphrates River

Syria

Lebanon

Mediterranean Sea

Palestine

Jordan River

Jerusalem

Dead Sea

Rosetta

Alexandria

Lower Egypt

Memphis

Sinai Peninsula

Arabia

Upper Egypt

Eastern Desert

Red Sea

Valley of the Kings

Thebes

Sahara

Abu Simbel

Nubia

Nile River

Kush

Old Kingdom (2700—2200 B.C.)

Middle Kingdom (2040—1674 B.C.)

New Kingdom (1552—1069 B.C.)

thority by dogma, which is another way of saying that his alone was the responsibility for the maintenance and nurture of his property. . . . Good government rested upon his success in bringing fertility to the soil, a profitable commerce, and the peace for normal internal development.[13]

A House of Ceremony

The pharaoh's residence was the most magnificent dwelling in Egypt, as befit a living symbol of the nation. Many Egyptian palaces were approached by royal roads, lined with small sphinxes or statues of protective jackals. Above the main entrance loomed a royal balcony, where the king showed himself to his subjects when the occasion demanded it. The palace itself was an entire complex of buildings, a city in miniature contained within protective gates and walls. (The royal palace was known as the *per ah*, or "great house." From this name writers in ancient times created the title of the king himself as "pharaoh.")

The main hall might contain antechambers and reception rooms as well as a throne room where the king or noble held audiences and handed down orders. Attached to the main hall were outbuildings that served as administrative offices, servants' quarters, women's quarters, storage facilities, and the like. Throughout, the halls were brightly painted with landscapes or scenes of daily life, showing the inhabitants hunting or feasting, their poses and profiles illuminated by the bright sunlight that flowed into the house from its high windows.

The pharaohs lived among beautifully worked sculptures, fine furniture made out of rare woods, and lush tapestries hanging from the walls. In the private apartments of the king, the individual rooms were high and spacious. Halls where the official business was

The unification of Egypt by Menes provided the Egyptians with their founding myth, a story of how the nation and its most important institution—the monarchy—came to be. Over the centuries, the historical facts were transformed into a titanic clash between the gods Horus and Seth. Christine Hobson, in *The World of the Pharaohs*, explains what may have been the facts behind this founding myth:

"In Upper Egypt, the town of Nubt near Naqada, dedicated to the god Seth, was ideally placed as a market centre. . . . Meanwhile to the south of Luxor, another town developed on the west bank of the Nile across from modern El Kab, known to ancient Egyptians as Nekhen. Its local god was the falcon Horus, giving rise to the Greek name for the site: Hieranconpolis (Falcon-city).

It was inevitable, given the new ambitions and the increasing wealth of Egypt, that these major centres should clash. According to many scholars, the very ancient story of the battles of Horus and Seth . . . was a folk-memory of the war that [was] waged between these two towns. The victory of Horus over Seth—that is, Hieranconpolis over Nubt—gave the prince of Hieranconpolis authority over the whole of Upper Egypt, and the power to extend and consolidate his territory until finally all Egypt was united under one king."

carried out were long and imposing. Artisans set glazed tiles highlighted with gold leaf on the floors and walls, and painters decorated the same surfaces with appropriate pictures of daily life and entertainment.

The Pharaoh's Daily Life

The dress of the king was strictly prescribed by tradition. The kings of Egypt wore dual white and red crowns as a symbol of the historic unification of Upper and Lower Egypt that had been brought about by Menes. They also wore long gowns and a symbolic bull's tail that hung from the belt. Another symbol of royal power was the uraeus, a protective female cobra that looked out from atop the king's headgear. Many portraits and sculptures of the kings show them carrying a shepherd's staff, a symbol of their role as guiders of the nation, and a flail or fly whisk, a symbol of their power to punish enemies both foreign and domestic.

Despite their power, the kings of ancient Egypt were not free. A king's every waking moment was scheduled according to custom and ceremony. Traditional religious rituals had to be performed each day; audiences were held at certain times and in certain places; even the words uttered by the king, and the speeches of those who had the authority to speak in his presence, were dictated by ancient formulas.

The king had many duties, all to be carried out according to time-honored tradition. For example, the king dedicated new buildings and temples and presided over religious rituals. He read documents and petitions brought to him by the vizier and other high officials. He also heard reports brought by his own diplomats and received important visitors from foreign lands. Through the reports of other officials, he kept close track of the

Nile flood and of the annual harvest of grain. The size of the harvest was of particular interest to the pharaoh, since it provided the people with an important measure of his success as a king.

From time to time, the king left his royal capital to inspect the principal cities of his realm. As commander-in-chief, he also visited frontier outposts and important military installations to review the troops and meet with officers. In time of war, he was responsible for deciding on the overall strategy of his armies. For the kings of Egypt as well as the local

Egyptian pharaohs wore a crown with a cobra ornament looking out from their headgear as a symbol of royal power.

princes known as nomarchs, a victory in battle was the highest achievement of all. On the occasion of one such defeat of a rival prince, one happy commander bragged,

> I spent the night on board my ship, my heart rejoicing, and when the day dawned I pounced on him like a hawk. I overthrew him at the moment when he was cleaning his teeth. I battered down his walls; I slaughtered his people; and I forced his wife to plunge down the bank of the river. My soldiers were like wolves with their prey.[14]

During the Middle Kingdom reign of Sesostris III, a large and permanent royal army was developed, intended to enforce the rule of the king and keep the country's nobility in check. The king of Egypt now assumed a new role, that of head of the army and conqueror of foreign lands. From the time of the Middle Kingdom, kings customarily led their troops into battle while riding in their royal chariots. On funerary artwork, the king was now celebrated as a great warrior whose royal power and semidivine status enabled him to subdue the troublesome Nubians of the south or the restless tribes from the northeast, who throughout Egypt's history wandered into the Delta, sometimes peacefully and sometimes not, to build their own cities and to settle on fertile land claimed from the Egyptians.

Celebrating the Reign

After thirty years of rule, tradition dictated that the kings should celebrate a great jubilee festival known as the *sed*, designed to renew and strengthen their bodies and their authority over the land. During the *sed*, an image of the aging king was ritually buried, while the king himself, magically transformed into his younger self, visited his domain to put on an exhibition of his physical strength and skills. The first *sed* festival was followed by others that took place every three or four years. Egyptologist Joyce Tyldesley explains,

> [It was] originally a public ceremony of rebirth intended to reaffirm the king's powers after each successive thirty years on the throne. However, kings who had achieved their first three decades felt free to bend the rules in subsequent years. As life expectancy at birth throughout the New Kingdom was less than twenty years, thirty years on the throne was by anyone's reckoning a remarkable achievement, and the celebration of an official jubilee gave the king and his people the excuse for a magnificent and lengthy party.[15]

For the ancient Egyptians, the *sed* festival was the traditional way to celebrate the power and longevity of their kings. These ceremonies lasted for many days and included great parades and feasts, a tour through the country by the king, and the king's ritual appearance before the populace at the doors of his palace. Preparations for the *sed* were often elaborate. For example, the jubilee of King Amenhotep III, celebrated in the fourteenth century B.C., included the construction of an immense ceremonial lake that measured two kilometers long by one kilometer wide, the largest earthwork of ancient Egypt, which can still be seen near the modern town of Birket Habu. Amenhotep's celebration was described in the Theban tomb of a high court official named Kheruef:

> The glorious appearance of the king at the great double doors in his palace, "The House of Rejoicing"; ushering in the officials, the king's friends, the chamberlain, the men of the gateway, the king's acquaintances, the crew of the barge, the castellans, and the king's dignitaries. Rewards were given out in the form of "Gold of Praise," and ducks and fish of gold, and they received ribbons of green linen, each person being made to stand according to his rank. They were fed with food as part

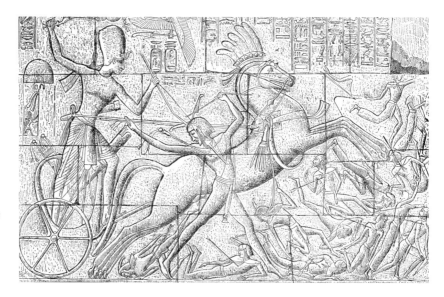

Egyptian kings, considered semi-divine in ancient Egypt, traditionally led their armies into battle while riding a chariot.

As part of the elaborate funeral ceremony, mummified corpses were often carried to their tombs on a funerary boat similar to this model.

of the king's breakfast: bread, beer, oxen, and fowl. They were directed to the lake of His Majesty to row in the king's barge. They grasped the towropes of the Evening Barge and the prow rope of the Morning Barge, and they towed the barges at the great place. They stopped at the steps of the throne.

It was His Majesty who did this in accordance with the writings of old . . . past generations of people since the time of the ancestors had never celebrated such jubilee rites.[16]

Monuments to the Dead Kings

No matter how popular or magical the festivals of rejuvenation, the king eventually passed on to the world of the dead. The Egyptians believed that the home of the dead played an important role in the passage to the afterlife, and by tradition the kings of Egypt had their own tombs prepared while they were still alive. Gangs of workers built the tombs underground, decorating them with paintings and stocking them with weapons, furniture, and other goods. In earliest times, the Egyptians placed small jars of food and drink be-

side the graves. Later, separate chambers were built to house the goods for the afterlife. So important were these goods thought to be that the produce of certain farming estates was dedicated solely to supplying the king's tomb for eternity. After the death of the king and the completion of the funeral ceremonies, the tombs were sealed against vandals and thieves.

The funeral ceremony was as elaborate as any carried out during a pharaoh's life. One such funeral ceremony is described in the book *Egypt: Land of the Pharaohs:*

Following the traditional 70-day ritual of embalming in the pharaoh's new capital of Pi-Ramses . . . the mummified body of Ramses would have been set aboard the lead vessel of a flotilla and conveyed up the Nile to Thebes. . . . On landing in Thebes, the mummy would be placed upon an ox-drawn sledge for the procession to the tomb. Led by shaven-headed priests chanting and wafting incense, the funeral train would wend its way into the Valley, its ranks swelled by professional mourners and servants carrying royal possessions. . . . At the entrance of the tomb, the royal bier would be greeted by ritual dancers, and by a priest who read funerary

During the symbolic rite of Opening the Mouth, the most important ceremony of an Egyptian funeral, the powers of speech, sight, and hearing were bestowed upon the mummy.

spells from a section of papyrus. Then would come the most important ceremony of the entire proceeding, the symbolic rite of Opening the Mouth. . . . The ritual's purpose was to bestow upon the mummy the powers of speech, sight, and hearing, restoring it to life for its existence in the beyond. . . .

This ritual completed, the departed pharaoh would receive offerings of clothing, incense, and food. The mourners, in turn, would partake of a funerary banquet. At the end of the festivities, the mummy was conveyed into the tomb and installed in the burial chamber. The footprints of the funeral party would be swept from the floor. Then the door to the tomb would be blocked with masonry, sealed, and covered with rubble, presumably closed forever.[17]

Near the king's resting place were raised tombs for the members of his family, for his administrators, for his court officials, and for friends and servants. In this way, the members of the court enjoyed proximity to the king and the privileges of their official positions even after death.

The Egyptian Nobles

While the king still lived, a vast array of royal administrators received his orders and saw to it that his will was carried out all through the land. These royal officials oversaw important state functions such as the collection of taxes, the raising of armies, and the building of public works and monuments. The head of one department oversaw the collection of surplus grain, which was stored in huge public granaries. This was, perhaps, one of the most important positions besides that of the pharaoh himself. According to Charles Freeman in *The Legacy of Ancient Egypt*,

The granaries owned by the state and the temples could be huge. The mortuary temple that Rameses II built for himself at Thebes, for instance, could store enough to feed perhaps 20,000 people for a year. The granaries were the "banks" of the state, with the grain its "capital" supporting the king's building projects.[18]

In the earliest dynasties, members of the king's own family carried out these duties. As time went on, however, a substantial class of officials and bureaucrats emerged to administer the Egyptian state. At the top of their class stood the vizier, the kingdom's "prime minister," who held a place second only to the king in authority and prestige. The vizier appeared before the king every day to make a report on the state of the realm. He had authority over public farming and irrigation projects, the mining of gold and gemstones, construction of public projects, finance, and the administration of justice. He was responsible for seeing that taxes were collected from farmers and landowners. He also oversaw the collection of tribute from foreign lands.

As the chief magistrate of Egypt, the vizier also saw that justice was carried out and crimes were punished. The Egyptians did not write down their laws, however. The vizier depended on custom and tradition, according to historian John Wilson:

> What the vizier dispensed was customary law, phrased as the commanding word of pharaoh and arising out of pharaoh's three divine qualities . . . of Authority, Perception, and Justice. Of course there were royal ordinances to fit specific instances, and of course there were precedents out of past judication, but . . . in Egypt, the law was personally derived from the god-king.[19]

Ancient Justice

The administration of law and order in ancient Egypt took some strange turns, at least in the view of modern readers. At first, historians speculate, justice was closely related to religious practice. If an item was stolen from a villager, for example, a list of all the inhabitants of a village would be read out before the statue of a god or a long-dead, deified king. When the thief's name was read out, the statue would make a sign. The accused could then make an appeal to another god, but if the first god still accused him, he would be beaten until he confessed. The ancient Egyptians, reports Erwin Seidl in Glanville's *The Legacy of Egypt*, "made [a] consistent attempt to build up a whole law of procedure upon the omniscience of the deity." Seidl continues,

"Criminal law and criminal procedure [in ancient Egypt] were inhuman. In contrast to Jewish law which limited corporal punishment to forty strokes, one hundred strokes was the ordinary punishment in Egypt. Torture was often used, not only upon the accused but also upon independent witnesses. Strange forms of capital punishment seem to have been practised, such as leaving the prisoner to be eaten by crocodiles. It was a special favour to allow a convicted criminal to commit suicide. Numbers of criminals, with their ears and noses cut off, were condemned to forced labour in concentration colonies on the frontiers of the country. A thief furthermore had to pay a multiple of the value of the stolen chattel [property]—a penalty which also can be paralleled in the Code of Hammurabi and in the oldest Roman law."

To keep control over the distant nomes (provinces), the king also appointed officials known as nomarchs. The nomarchs came from among the wealthiest and most powerful local families. They had small palaces of their own, which held departments of taxes, courts of justice, and offices for scribes and bureaucrats. The nomarch's power was of a highly personal nature, since he had almost daily contact with the people over whom he ruled. Moreover, he served as the high priest at local temples and held the command of a local army.

The kings paid their loyal nomarchs in the form of grants of lands and titles in hopes of retaining their loyalty. But the power of the nomarchs proved to be a constant concern to the king's own ministers. In several cases, disobedient nomarchs usurped the king's authority and became independent rulers in their own right, governing their nomes in defiance of a king whose capital might be several weeks' sailing time away.

During the First Intermediate Period, a time when disloyal independent nomarchs plunged Egypt into many years of civil war, the country's administration changed. Members of the artisan class were recruited, trained, and accepted into the ranks of the royal officials. They might begin as tax collectors, policemen, soldiers, scribes, magistrates, or minor priests. By showing ability and loyalty to the monarch, they advanced in rank and authority, with a few attaining high positions. It was even possible to rise above humble origins to take a place at the king's side as an official of the royal court. In his book *Egypt of the Pharaohs*, historian Sir Alan Gardiner translates one inscription by a man of humble birth named Weni, who lived during the reign of Pepi I (2338–2298 B.C.). Weni had the following account of his life written on the walls of his tomb at the city of Abydos:

Whilst I was a magistrate, His Majesty [King Pepi I] made me a Sole Friend and Overseer of the tenants of the Palace, and I displaced four Overseers of the tenants of the Palace who were there, and I acted to His Majesty's satisfaction in giving escort, in preparing the king's path, and in taking up courtly positions, I doing all so that His Majesty praised me for it beyond anything.

During the First Intermediate Period, artisans were trained to fill many jobs, some becoming scribes, as depicted here. If successful in these positions, they often advanced in rank and authority.

When His Majesty inflicted punishment upon the Asiatics and Sand-dwellers, His Majesty made an army of many tens of thousands from the entire [land of] Upper Egypt. . . . It was I who was in command of them, though my office was [merely] that of an Overseer of the tenants of the Palace, because I was well suited to prevent one from quarrelling with his fellow, to prevent any one of them from taking bread or sandals from a wayfarer, to prevent any one of them from taking a loin-cloth from any village, to prevent any one of them from taking any goat from any [person]. . . . This army returned in peace, it had slain troops in it many tens of thousands.[20]

In the King's Shadow

During their lifetimes, viziers, nomarchs, and other nobles gained prestige by winning the favor of the king. The pharaohs rewarded loyalty by allowing their lands and titles to pass on to their descendants when they died. Still, to keep tabs on the nomarch, a royal commissioner, a member of the king's own court, lived in each nome. There were also royal overseers who managed the land and herds that belonged to the king.

Late in ancient Egyptian history, the nation's social classes became more isolated from one another as growing numbers of professional administrators and mercenaries made up a powerful class of bureaucrats that kept the ordinary Egyptian peasants and artisans from rising above their stations in life. According to historian John A. Wilson,

The hired professional factor [manager] stood between the ruling, wealthy class and the ordinary mass of Egyptians; there was

no longer that regular and easy contact between the master and his peasants. There was a class cleavage, and it was no longer possible—theoretically and exceptionally—to move upward in the social scale. The high value set upon the individual Egyptian, down to the ordinary peasant, in the early Middle Kingdom was a thing of the distant past. Under the Empire the peasant was only an indistinguishable element in the mass of Egyptians organized and restrained for national united effort.[21]

The Noble's Life

The aristocrats of ancient Egypt lived well. One text, used by young people while learning to write hieroglyphs, describes the daily routine of the upper crust of Egyptian society:

You go down to your ship of fir-wood, manned from bow to stern. You reach your beautiful villa, the one you have built for yourself. Your mouth is full of wine and beer, of bread, meat, and cakes. Oxen are slaughtered and melodious singing is before you. Your chief anointer anoints you with ointment of gum. Your manager of cultivated land bears garlands. Your chief fowler brings ducks, your fisherman brings fish. Your ship has returned from Syria laden with all manner of good things.[22]

The nobility lived in large homes in imitation of the comfort and majesty of the royal palace. Their estates might spread across two or three acres, surrounded by a high and thick protective wall. The houses themselves rose two or more stories above ground level and contained ten or twenty rooms, which included reception halls, banquet halls, bedrooms, and private quarters. Bathrooms were built over

Made of ebony and elaborately decorated, this ceremonial chair most likely belonged to an Egyptian noble.

The houses of the nobles and the well-to-do were furnished with chests, stools, armchairs, beds, and tables (instead of long tables for the entire company, dining halls were made up of several small tables around which a few people ate their repast). The best furniture was carefully worked out of expensive imported wood and inlaid with precious stones, gold, or silver. On the floor were spread mats woven from reeds and thick cushions for the comfort of guests. Although most Egyptians slept on simple rush mats, the well-to-do provided themselves with beds made with wicker stretched over a four-legged wooden frame. Their bedrooms might have wooden cupboards to hold clothes, shoes, gloves, and linens.

A staff of servants, artisans, cooks, and others saw to the maintenance of the house. Servants wove clothing, baked bread, maintained gardens and pools, made repairs, swept floors, served meals, and waited on the family. Servants also accompanied their master outside the house, shading him with heavy canopies and shooing away flies with elaborate whisks. The servant's job was to make the master comfortable.

There are very few instances of rebellious or resentful servants in ancient Egyptian painting or writing. Every individual had his or her appointed and natural place in society, a place that was accepted and endured. That went for all strata of society, even the skilled professionals—such as scribes and doctors—who saw to the nation's day-to-day routines.

drainage pipes that led outside the walls of the estate. The large courtyards where families and servants spent much of their time held gardens with orchards, flower beds, rectangular pools, and a scattering of small shrines. Several rooms or a large main hall might be dedicated to banqueting or entertainment, for it was an important duty of the nobles to put on great feasts and banquets and to hire musicians and dancers for special occasions.

CHAPTER 3

In the Service of the Pharaoh: Scribes, Doctors, Soldiers, and Slaves

The pharaoh of Egypt represented the entire nation, and in turn the entire nation of Egypt worked in his service. In this way, the everyday tasks carried out by ordinary people all made up a single, immense community effort, devoted to the greater glory of a single human being. These tasks were carefully prescribed by rules and traditions, learned while a youngster was still under instruction from parents and teachers. Up and down the Nile valley, there were hundreds of roles to fill and functions to carry out, but the most essential jobs were carried out by four classes: scribes, doctors, soldiers, and slaves.

The Schooling of a Scribe

The children of scribes were expected to follow in the footsteps of their fathers. These children enjoyed the privilege of a secure future, but they were also subjected to a harsh condemnation if their parents were found disobedient, dishonest, or incompetent (the children of banished officials were sometimes turned into ordinary laborers, even slaves).

At the age of four or five, some Egyptian boys began attending school, which lasted until the students were taken into their apprenticeships (girls did not attend school but might apprentice to a profession that was open to them). The most important goal of schooling in ancient Egypt was to teach boys to read and write. The Egyptians understood literacy as the passport to an easy life, the key to advancement, and the chance for a place in the sought-after profession of scribe.

Students learned the hieroglyphic alphabet (used for religious and political inscriptions), practicing their marks with reed brushes on rolls of papyrus or on pieces of stone or *ostraka* (pottery fragments). They also learned the hieratic script, used for everyday correspondence. The teacher dictated stories and poems, and the students dutifully wrote down what they heard. Watched over by a master who was ready at any minute with a switch or stick to inflict punishment, the students copied out texts on pieces of broken pottery and were given long lessons in history, geography, mathematics, and other subjects. In schools where it was appropriate, they also studied arithmetic. Foreign languages such as Akkadian, the diplomatic language of the region, might be studied in government schools.

At all levels, children were taught respect for their elders and politeness in the presence of strangers. Infractions of rules and poor behavior were punished with a lash or stick. Moral teaching was given through the examples and sayings of wise men of the past. The greatest emphasis in the Egyptian school was on learning one's proper place in a rigid social hierarchy.

At some royal schools, native Egyptian students may have worked and studied alongside

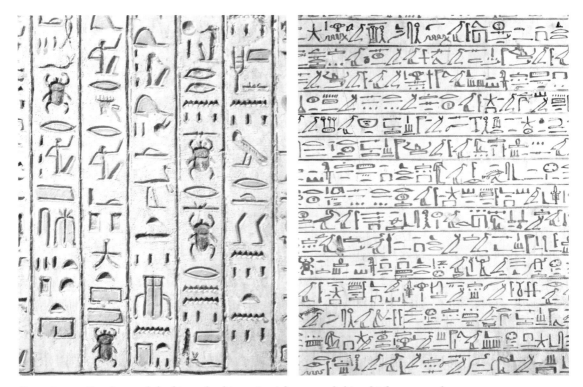

Egyptian scribes learned the hieroglyphic script (shown on left), which was used for religious and political inscriptions, and the hieratic script (shown on right), which was used for everyday correspondence.

the sons of foreigners. This was brought about by a carefully calculated Egyptian foreign policy. In her book *Nefertiti,* Joyce Tyldesley explains that

> Egypt was in the habit of demanding that the sons of vassals and allies be sent to Egypt for their education. These young men, educated alongside the Egyptian princes in the school attached to the royal harem, served as hostages who would ensure the good behaviour of their fathers. They became so steeped in Egyptian customs and beliefs that, when they returned to rule their own countries, their loyalties in theory lay not with their own people but with the Egyptian king who had become their friend.[23]

The Professional Scribe

Scribes held one of the most prestigious niches in all Egyptian society. Through their ability to record and communicate in writing, scribes allowed the complex administration of a far-flung kingdom to function. Using papyrus, a long, thin roll of linen-like material, scribes wrote letters and prepared official records and legal documents. Working in villages where the entire population might be illiterate, they served as the people's direct link to their government. They created inventories of goods, tracking the stores of the king or the nobles for whom they worked. They recorded the payment of taxes, trading in land and property, the decisions of Egyptian magistrates, the weight of harvests, and the rolls of army conscripts.

They also copied out stories and poems for leisure-time enjoyment by those people who could read and enjoy literature.

The working methods of the Egyptian scribe are described by Christine Hobson in *The World of the Pharaohs*:

> With the papyrus roll in his left hand, the scribe either stood, sat cross-legged or occasionally squatted at a low desk to write. . . . Over his shoulder he would have a strap; at the front would be suspended an ink-palette, and at the back, a pen-holder and a small water pot. Two indentations in the ink-palette contained small discs of ink—black, made from carbon, and red, from ochre—mixed with gum and allowed to harden. Using a brush-pen made from a softened maritime reed the scribe would moisten his brush in the water pot, dab it into the ink, and paint, rather than write, with his hand suspended over the surface of the papyrus.[24]

The scribe could carry out his function nearly anywhere. He might have a permanent chamber or a work room in his home. Statues and paintings show scribes working while sitting cross-legged, gradually unrolling the papyrus as they continue. The roll of papyrus was used until it was completely filled; it was then rolled up into a small tube, tied, and added to a

In Praise of Scribes

The place of the scribe was a place of honor in Egyptian society. It was recognized by all that the scribe played a crucial role in guaranteeing the smooth functioning, prosperity, and continuity of the kingdom. To encourage young men to join this profession, an entire literary genre developed to praise the joys and comforts of the scribing life.

One of these works from the Middle Kingdom, known as *The Satire of the Trades* (quoted by editor David Silverman in his book *Ancient Egypt*), provides a vivid description of the hard life lived by those unfortunates who grew up as something other than scribes.

"I have seen a coppersmith at his work, at the mouth of his furnace,
His fingers like the claws of a crocodile, and he stinks worse than fish roe.

Every carpenter who wields the adze, he is wearier than the laborer in the field.
His field is the wood, and his hoe the axe.
There is no end to his craft, and he does beyond what his arms are capable of. . . .

The jeweller is boring carefully into every type of hard stone.
He completes the inlay of an eye, his arms are exhausted and he is weary.
He sits at sunset, with his knees and his back cramped. . . .

The potter is under the soil, although he stands among the living.
He grubs in the mud more than a pig in order to bake his pots.
His clothes are stiff with clay, his loincloth in rags.
Breath enters his nose direct from his furnace.
He tramples [the clay] with his feet, and is himself crushed by it."

bundle that was carried in a small leather or wooden case. The scribe also owned a small case for his ink and writing instruments, and with this, he could travel from one nome or kingdom to the next, wherever duty called him.

The most accomplished scribes of ancient Egypt learned to draw hieroglyphs. Hieroglyphs were a system of picture writing that consisted of ideograms (symbolizing ideas) and sound symbols. Eventually, twenty-four different hieroglyphs were developed to represent single consonant sounds, and several more were created for consonant combinations (vowels were not represented in hieroglyphic script).

In addition, scribes learned to use hieratic script, or "priestly writing," a simpler form of hieroglyphs. Scribes, as well as literate nobles and artisans, used hieratic script for everyday letters and records. Royal and provincial officials used hieratic script for official correspondence, orders, written decrees, and the like. Later in their history, the ancient Egyptians invented a demotic, or "popular," script that was a simpler version of hieratic. An even larger segment of the population could use demotic script for their records and letters.

Medicine

The ancient Egyptians believed that the hieroglyphs used by skilled scribes had a religious basis. The ability to create such symbols gave the scribe a high status in Egyptian society. The religion of ancient Egypt also formed an important basis for the practice of medicine, and as a result the doctors of ancient Egypt enjoyed high status as well.

Although prosperous, ancient Egypt was not always a healthy place to live. Historian Charles Freeman comments,

> The Egyptians were no more immune to illness than any other people. . . . The average lifespan was only 29 years, but this reflected the high infant mortality. Those who did survive all the hazards of early life might expect to reach 50. Diseases of the lungs, caused by tuberculosis and the breathing of sand and dust, were common. So were parasites, absorbed from polluted water. The teeth of mummies appear worn down, probably as a result of chewing grit left in grain after it had been ground. Those who survived by 40 usually had worn and, doubtless, painful joints and showed evidence of strained spines.[25]

Egyptian doctors began training in their craft at an early age. While serving as apprentices to experienced doctors, students learned surgical techniques, how to set broken bones, and the use of splints, bandages, and plaster

Scribes generally painted with reed brushes on rolls of papyrus, seen here, or on pieces of stone or ostraka *(pottery).*

casts. They applied balms and ointments to external wounds, cuts, and burns and carried out cosmetic surgery on those wishing to appear young again.

Patients were thoroughly examined and questioned before a diagnosis was given, after which the doctor would make the decision either to treat or not treat the patient. The Egyptians treated illnesses with a combination of magic spells and medicine, often using revolting substances that were ingested to drive away the evil influences believed to bring about sickness. The Egyptians wrote down their medicine and prescriptions on papyri, some of which give techniques of surgery and incantations meant for the healing of injury or illness. The ancient Egyptians also compiled lists of anatomical and other medical terms. Ancient Egyptian medical practices were documented in what is now known as the Edwin Smith Papyrus, a text that explains the proper treatment and care of forty-eight different injuries.

Among the ancient Egyptians, illness was seen as a manifestation of the loss of balance in one's life that was expressed in the physical body. If the cause of the illness was unknown or not apparent, the Egyptian doctor blamed it on an unhappy deity or perhaps bad magic performed by a human enemy. Injuries or chronic illnesses could also be blamed on a transgression against the gods. When one workman named Neferabu, who lived at the workers' community of Deir el-Medina in western Thebes, suddenly went blind, he left the following inscription on his funeral stela in explanation:

I am a man who swore falsely by Ptah,
    Lord of Truth;
and he caused me to see darkness in
    daylight.
I shall proclaim his power to the one

The Edwin Smith Papyrus

The Edwin Smith Papyrus, named after an American Egyptologist, is one of the world's first medical textbooks. It dates from around 1700 B.C., but most of the information is based on even older texts written around 2640 B.C. The papyrus deals with the treatment of forty-eight different kinds of wounds and medical conditions, starting with injuries to the head and working down to the rest of the body. One section of the papyrus, quoted in a website called "The Page of Egyptian Medicine," recommends the following treatment for "stupid [poor] vision":

"Take the water (humor) contained in pigs eyes, take true antimony, red lead, natural honey, of each 1 Ro (about 15 cc); pulverize it finely and combine it into one mass which should be injected into the ear of the patient and he will be cured immediately. Do and thou shalt see. Really excellent! Thou shalt recite as a spell: I have brought this which was applied to the seat of yonder and replaces the horrible suffering. Twice."

who does not know him, and the one
    who does,
To the small and great.
Beware of Ptah, Lord of Truth!
He will not overlook the deed of any
    man.
Beware of uttering the name of Ptah
    falsely;
Lo, he who utters it falsely,
He is cast down.[26]

When the doctors of ancient Egypt could not heal, they resorted to magic. For example, the baleful actions of evil spirits or the dead were sometimes blamed for an illness. Especially suspect were the actions of Sekhmet, the bloody-minded lion-headed goddess who lived at the edge of the desert, bringing disease and destruction to humans. To treat illness, the spirits were attacked with spells and incantations. If a certain deceased individual was suspected as the perpetrator of the problem, his or her tomb might be attacked and desecrated or destroyed, which Egyptians believed would kill the wandering, baleful soul of the deceased once and for all.

Whether or not these treatments worked, the Egyptians enjoyed a reputation as the finest medical doctors in the world. Egyptians traveled all over the ancient world to heal the nobles and kings of distant lands; the sick or injured arrived in Egyptian cities to seek out doctors who worked in the service of the royal court and temples.

Life in the Egyptian Army

Being a physician or a scribe offered prestige and a secure life, but in Egypt's highly stratified society these jobs were open to few individuals, mostly men whose fathers had been in the same profession. For other young men, particularly in later centuries after Egypt had grown rich and powerful, the military offered an equal opportunity for advancement.

For much of its history, Egypt had little need for a professional standing army. The nation occupied a narrow and easily defended valley; on the north lay a great sea, and on the east and west stretched vast, dry deserts that could not sustain large enemy forces. Instead of a permanent national army, the king drafted soldiers from each nome for the purpose of defense in times of need. Within the nomes, each governor controlled his own local army, which was often secondary to other concerns. During

This statue depicts the goddess Sekhmet, who was believed to bring disease and destruction to humans.

the Fourth Dynasty, for example, powerful monarchs spent their kingdom's resources on building pyramids, not on military campaigns. Historian Lionel Casson describes the Egyptian military of that time:

> The army was largely a kind of feudal levy that was called upon only in time of need. The pharaoh might keep a small cadre of standing troops, but in an emergency he called upon the provincial nobles to conscript the peasants who normally tended the fields, the canals and quarries. He put them under the command of a royal son or a member of the nobility, and sent them off to fight for as long as the emergency lasted. When the trouble passed, the levied men would return to their plows and their benches.[27]

In later times, when Egypt became a great military power, a standing army was created. Thousands of volunteers joined the military for money, land, servants, and career advancement. The army offered opportunity; rather than spending a short life within the ranks, ordinary soldiers could rise to higher-ranking positions: standard bearers who led infantry regiments, fortress commanders, and regimental commanders. These officers, in turn, could rise within the royal administration to become one of the king's military advisers—or all the way up, as is recorded several times in Egypt's history, to the king's throne.

Professional soldiers in Egypt were trained from boyhood in the skills of marching, drilling, and fighting. The life of a soldier in training was brutal, and it improved little when the individual set out on campaign. According to one ancient text, quoted by Pierre Montet,

> Come, listen to my stories of his campaigns in Syria, of his marches over the mountains. He carries his bread and his water on his shoulder like an ass's burden; his spine is dislocated. He drinks brackish water and sleeps with one eye open. When he encounters the enemy he is like a bird caught in a snare and there is no strength left in his limbs. When the time comes for him to return to Egypt he is like a worm-eaten piece of wood. He is ill, paralysis seizes him and he has to be led on a donkey. His clothes have been filched by robbers and his orderly takes to his heels.[28]

Ancient Egypt's military reflected the rest of society: Foot soldiers came from the class of peasants and artisans, while chariot regiments were made up of members of the nobility, who equipped their own chariots, horses, and drivers. The infantry regiments also included foreign mercenaries who came from among the Libyans, Nubians, and, late in Egyptian history, Greeks.

The Egyptian foot soldier wore a short skirt, woven out of coarse linen, and a small leather shield over the abdomen. Through most of Egypt's history, there were no helmets or armor to protect the head and body. Pay consisted of a daily ration of food, and on campaign, soldiers shared in any loot captured from an enemy city. Officers who performed well in battle were rewarded with medals and insignia that they hung from small chains around their necks.

The Egyptian army divisions contained about five thousand men. Each division was named after a god. Within the division were infantry regiments and chariot squadrons, which included about twenty-five chariots each. The chariots were drawn by two horses and had two occupants: the soldier himself and the driver. At the start of the battle, it was the charioteers' job to gallop in front of the enemy lines, hurling javelins and spears to

Although soldiers endured a brutally difficult life, many Egyptians joined the military to obtain money, land, servants, and potential career advancement.

soften the resistance of the enemy. Archers stood at a distance, using bows made of wood, horn, and sinew to send a deadly hail of arrows into the enemy ranks. The infantry followed, closing with the enemy and attacking in mass with their spears, axes, and daggers. The infantryman had only the slight protection of a leather shield, strung over a wooden frame, against the enemy's weapons.

A victorious effort by the Egyptian armies meant great herds of enemy captives, among whom a few would be ritually executed to symbolize the victory and to provide the survivors with a demonstration of Egyptian might. On the walls of a temple dedicated to himself, the mighty pharaoh Ramses II described one such victory over the Hittites at the Battle of Kadesh:

> I dashed at them like the god of war; I massacred them, slaughtering them where they stood while one shrieked to the other, "This is no man, but a mighty god; those are not the deeds of man; never has one man thus overcome hundreds of thousands!" I slew them all; none escaped me. . . . I caused the field of Kadesh to be white with corpses, so that one did not know where to tread because of their multitude. I fought all alone and overcame the foreigners in their millions.[29]

The survivors would then be recorded by the army scribes, who tabulated human as well as animal captives—sheep, goats, cattle, and horses—and weapons and supplies taken from the enemy. To provide an exact count of the enemy dead, one hand was severed from each corpse and tallied by military bookkeepers. The spoils of the battle were transported to the king and presented in a ritual at which the victory was dedicated to Amon, the reigning god of New Kingdom Egypt.

During the New Kingdom, the Egyptians also made use of ships, which carried infantry and archers along the Mediterranean coast in support of the troops fighting on land. Skilled boatbuilders, the ancient Egyptians equipped their ships with sails as well as two banks of oars, lending the vessels speed and maneuverability. These vessels were also used as a means of coastal defense and in peacetime as trading vessels. From time to time, the king would send his ships on raiding expeditions intended to gather needed material and captives to fight for the pharaohs during their land campaigns.

Slaves

If the army was necessary to extend and maintain the pharaoh's power, slaves were essential to the management of the great households of the pharaohs and nobility. In ancient Egypt,

The Battle of Megiddo, 1469 B.C.

Ramses II was credited by his people as being a great military leader. An account of one great battle Ramses fought against the Hittites appears in the "Internet Ancient History Sourcebook":

"Then was set up the camp of his majesty, and command was given to the whole army, saying: 'Equip yourselves! Prepare your weapons! for we shall advance to fight with that wretched foe in the morning.' Therefore the king rested in the royal tent, the affairs of the chiefs were arranged, and the provisions of the attendants. The watch of the army went about, saying, 'Steady of heart! Steady of heart! Watchful! Watchful! Watch for life at the tent of the king.' One came to say to his majesty, 'The land is well, and the infantry of the South and North likewise.'

Year 23 [of the king's reign], first month of the third season, on the twenty-first day, the day of the feast of the new moon, corresponding to the royal coronation, early in the morning, behold, command was given to the entire army to move. His majesty went forth in a chariot of electrum, arrayed in his weapons of war, like Horus, the Smiter, lord of power; like Montu of Thebes, while his father, Amon, strengthened his arms. The southern wing of this army of his majesty was on a hill south of the brook of Kina, the northern wing was at the northwest of Megiddo, while his majesty was in their center, with Amon as the protection of his mem-

bers, the valor of his limbs. Then his majesty prevailed against them at the head of his army, and when they saw his majesty prevailing against them they fled headlong to Megiddo in fear, abandoning their horses and their chariots of gold and silver. The people hauled them up, pulling them by their clothing, into this city; the people of this city having closed it against them and lowered clothing to pull them up into this city. Now, if only the army of his majesty had not given their heart to plundering the things of the enemy, they would have captured Megiddo at this moment, when the wretched foe of Kadesh and the wretched foe of this city were hauled up in haste to bring them into this city. The fear of his majesty had entered their hearts, their arms were powerless, his serpent diadem was victorious among them.

Then were captured their horses, their chariots of gold and silver were made spoil, their champions lay stretched out like fishes on the ground. The victorious army of his majesty went around counting their portions. Behold, there was captured the tent of that wretched foe in which was his son. The whole army made jubilee, giving praise to Amon for the victory which he had granted to his son on this day, giving praise to his majesty, exalting his victories. They brought up the booty which they had taken, consisting of hands, of living prisoners, of horses, chariots of gold and silver."

slaves were known as "listeners" (because they listened for their orders), as "cupbearers," or as "followers." The slaves and household servants of Egypt came from captives from battles, from immigrating foreigners who were sold into slavery, or from people who had to sell themselves to escape poverty or to pay their debts. (Criminals could also be enslaved and put to work in the mines of the Eastern Desert, a career from which few returned alive, or simply exiled as permanent outcasts in the desert oases, where disease, Bedouin raids, and the scarcity of fertile land and water made for a hard and usually very short life.)

There was no lack of work for an Egyptian household servant. He might have the job of providing chairs, shoes, or floor mats for the master whenever needed or of bringing food and drink when demanded. Women slaves might be called on to perform music or to dance at banquets and feasts. In addition, women slaves looked after children and livestock, kept pools and gardens watered, swept out chambers and hallways, and dealt with merchants who came calling.

Slaves could be sold or lent by their owners. They could also be sent on dangerous and illegal errands such as tomb robbing, which was taken up by some unscrupulous nobles in search of gold and valuable artifacts. If caught at this task, the slave who once lived in an aristocratic household could be banished to a much harder life in the mines and quarries of the Eastern Desert or the Sinai. Here they labored in brutal conditions, suffering hunger, thirst, and the threat of beatings and whippings by their overseers.

Ironically, slaves had more social mobility than many free Egyptians. Most household servants could at least rise to free status; some married into the household they served and thus were freed. According to historian John A. Wilson,

While slaves serving in aristocratic households often lived better than free peasants, slaves working in mines and quarries remained under the constant threat of beatings and starvation.

Slavery was not then the sharply and legally delimited category which it was in more modern times. The household slave was much better off than the native Egyptian peasant. As the leg-man for a government bureau, as the body-servant of a noble, as an attendant in the royal harem, or as the sergeants in a mercenary detachment, the slave had greater opportunity to make himself indispensable and thus powerful.[30]

The skills learned by the household slave could also allow him to rise to the rank of artisan, a worker who created items in stone, wood, or metal. As an artisan, the average Egyptian could assure himself a good and steady living, for he was never dependent on the flood of the Nile or the whims of a king for his livelihood. The artisan class of Egypt held firmly onto the middle rungs of the social ladder, for their skills and knowledge provided the rest of society with the goods that made life easier and more civilized.

CHAPTER 4

Egyptian Art and Artisans

To live in the Nile valley in ancient times was to live in a secure and isolated region, a world not dependent on or fearful of neighbors. Ancient Egyptians saw their kingdom as the center of the world and the best place on earth; their gods ruled in the heavens and their society represented the summit of human achievement. Their art and architecture developed independently, without the influence of new styles from Asia, Europe, or other parts of Africa, and their furniture, jewelry, pottery, and other craft goods remained uniquely Egyptian. From the time of their youthful apprenticeships, Egyptian artisans were instructed in the proper techniques to carry out their work, learning all the time that the Egyptian way was the right way and the best way.

A skilled artisan was a valued member of Egyptian society. The king and the nobility recognized their dependence on the masons, painters, and sculptors who created their luxurious palaces and elaborate tombs. After all, only these anonymous laborers had the knowledge and skill to raise the mastabas and small pyramids placed in the vicinity of the king's own royal pyramid. They carved the inscriptions to warn away trespassers and tomb robbers, curses that brought the gods down on anyone defiling the eternal resting places. They painted the scenes of feasting and hunting on the walls of the tombs, creating the paradise that would magically materialize after the tomb was sealed and its occupant prepared to enjoy a happy eternity.

The Artisan Class

The artisans of ancient Egypt made up a "middle class" of stonemasons, sculptors, painters, cabinetmakers, goldsmiths, carpenters, jewelers, and so forth. Most Egyptian artisans belonged to workshops that specialized in producing a particular article, such as paintings, statuary, jewelry, or weaponry. A single workshop might have dozens of laborers who worked under the eyes and orders of an overseer. The most highly skilled artisans worked independently out of their homes, where one room was set aside as a studio. Others entered the service of a wealthy household, and still others spent their days traveling from one city to the next, making their skills available to whoever might need them.

Many Egyptian artisans were drafted for work on public projects such as royal tombs, temples, monuments, and pyramids. As such, they were considered servants of the king himself, and their work records were carefully kept by the king's vast army of dutiful scribes. The following account describes work on one public project:

> Leaving their village homes, the craftsmen would file through the single gateway in the wall and march off for a prescribed period of labor at the latest tomb site. There they lived in small stone huts for eight days, after which they got two days off to go home. As each laborer reported to the tomb, his arrival was

This mural (ca. 1550–1295 B.C.) depicts jewelers, members of the artisan class of ancient Egypt.

noted by the scribe on an attendance sheet, like a modern factory worker's timecard. Occasionally an artisan would miss work, and then as now the excuses could be quite inventive. "Eye trouble" and "brewing beer" were popular alibis.[31]

Some artisans escaped the everyday toil of the workshops and attained careers as independent contractors. They earned more money by working on private commissions granted by the nobles and those wealthy families who could afford them. The artisans might create sculpture for a noble's courtyard or paint scenes for the walls of bedchambers and feasting halls within the house. A few of the wealthiest Egyptians had artisans working and living within their own estates as permanent employees. These laborers stood ready to carry out any needed work in stone or metal.

Egyptian artisans passed their techniques on to their sons, who were expected to follow the professions practiced by their fathers. Their training began early in life, and most sons of artisans spent no time in school (since the skills of reading and writing were unnecessary to their future trade). It was common for many generations of a single family to be engaged in the same trade. In some cases, their names might be associated with a unique style or technique that characterized the products of a certain village or region.

Egyptian artisans achieved beauty as well as utility in the objects they created—the result of centuries of practice and experimentation. Charles Freeman comments,

> These achievements are even more remarkable in light of the fact that Egyptian tools remained primitive. The pyramids were built using raw manpower, mallets, chisels, ramps and sleds. The wheel was known by the New Kingdom, but was impractical to use on sand. Stone knives continued to be used alongside copper and bronze even when these metals became available. Iron was the last metal to be developed; it was more scarce than gold.[32]

Following Tradition

For the most part, artisans followed traditional techniques that remained unchanged over the

Pyramids were the most enduring contributions of ancient Egyptian architects and stonemasons. Here, an artist's rendering depicts the construction of a pyramid.

Egyptian Art and Artisans

centuries. The painters of Egypt, for example, all worked from identical patterns and used rigidly fixed proportions for human and divine figures. These patterns were rendered by drawing a rectangular grid on the surface to be painted, then carefully sketching the figures in the correct proportions over this grid. Charles Freeman describes the technique:

> A grid was drawn up . . . and the figure arranged so that the hairline was 18 units high, the shoulders were six units across, the arm from elbow to fingertip was 4.5 units and the foot 3 units long. If the figure was to be shown sitting, the same proportions were used, but the part of the grid relating to the thigh bone was placed horizontally. Similar grids were used when drawing animals.[33]

Egyptian figures were always shown with the head and legs in profile and the body facing frontally—an ideal rendering, to the artists' way of thinking, of all the essential features of the body. In the art from ancient times, larger figures indicate a higher status; smaller figures represent children, servants, or slaves.

Like painters, sculptors followed strict rules and traditions for their art. Instead of creating a likeness of the subject, the Egyptian sculptor attempted to create an ideal— a human figure in a state of perfection. He worked to carve the head, trunk, arms, and legs in certain proportions to each other and always tried to closely match both sides of the face, eliminating the slight variations between the two sides of the subject's face. Sculptors began with a rough block in stone, which was then marked with a sketch of the subject and carefully cut out of the rock with simple chisels, hammers, and saws.

Jewelers worked with semiprecious stones, in gold or silver, in lapis lazuli from mines in central Asia, in green stones such as malachite or beryl, and in turquoise, carnelian, and rock crystal. They cut the stones to preferred shapes and sizes, then ground them down to achieve a shiny polish. The stones were set in earrings, bracelets, armlets, and pectorals (pieces that were suspended over the wearer's chest).

One of the most common forms of jewelry in ancient Egypt was the protective amulet, which was worn in a strand around the neck. These came in various shapes and colors, each having a certain significance. The Eye of Horus warded off evil and brought healing; the Djed amulet, which resembled a tower, brought strength and stability; the Ankh amulet symbolized life. Certain colors also carried certain meanings: red for power, blue for protection, and green for happiness.

Working in Wood, Metal, and Glass

Egyptian carpenters provided many of the finer and more important things of life: furniture, chests, headrests for sleeping, and, of course, coffins for the repose of the dead. The carpenter had a wide variety of materials and tools available. Imported wood included cedar and cypress from Lebanon and ebony brought by caravan from central Africa. Native trees were sparse in the Nile valley, but there were several very useful varieties present:

> For roofing beams the carpenter could use either the date palm or the doom palm. Pegs and dowels for coffins and furniture could be made from acacia; walking sticks were cut from tamarisk trees. One of the best local woods was the sycamore fig, out of which coffins, tables, cosmetic chests, and statues were made.[34]

Potters and metalsmiths created many utensils for daily Egyptian life, such as the small bowl, wine flask, wine cup, bronze dagger, and gold ornaments shown here.

The Egyptian metalsmith provided the most useful objects for rich as well as poor customers. Before the time of the Old Kingdom, they were creating household utensils such as cooking pots, small jars, and knives, and other objects out of copper that was mined from quarries in the Sinai Peninsula. Later, the Egyptians learned how to create heavier and harder bronze by melting down copper and tin and mixing them into an alloy. Bronze goods were highly valued until the New Kingdom, when the Egyptian armies found themselves at a disadvantage when faced with the iron weapons of the Assyrians and other tribes to the east. (Eventually, the Egyptians also adopted the use of iron, but it was too late to prevent the kingdom's conquest by the Persians in the first millennium B.C.)

Around 1500 B.C., Egyptian artisans also learned the process for making glass. The ancient glassmaker heated, melted, and shaped sand into thin rods of colored glass that could be combined into small containers for valuable perfumes and oils. Jewelers used small glass balls to decorate jewelry, and later in Egyptian history merchants used simple glass vessels to store their most perishable goods. Glass remained a rare commodity, however, and glassmaking a skill known to only a few artisans.

Among the most numerous Egyptian artisans were the potters, who supplied an essential item to all households. Potters worked with the Nile River's abundant clay, which could be easily collected. They worked out lumps in the clay by kneading it with their hands or feet and then threw the clay on a simple wooden wheel. Potters created plates, vases, jars, cups, bowls, pitchers, wine and beer jugs, and dozens of other useful items. The finished pieces were painted with borders, patterns, nature scenes, or other artwork that would make the utensil, no matter how mundane its use, more beautiful and valuable in the eyes of its owner.

Whereas potters, painters, and sculptors might work for anyone or even be self-employed, all goldsmiths worked in shops

The first pyramid, the 204-foot-high tomb for the Pharaoh Djoser, was designed in seven courses or "steps" of stone by the architect Imhotep. The Step Pyramid is the oldest stone building in the world.

that belonged to the king. The ancient Egyptians mined gold in Nubia or in the Eastern Desert and then transported the gold under heavy guard to the workshops, where it could be melted down and cast or hammered into shape. Finished gold objects and jewelry went straight to the king's treasury rooms, where it was bestowed on deserving Egyptians by the king himself in payment for faithful service.

Architects and Stonemasons

Of all Egyptian artisans, however, none were more valued than the architects and masons who built the pyramids, the lasting symbol of Egypt. The essential purpose of pyramids was to serve as protective tombs and monuments for the Egyptian kings. For the rulers of the Old Kingdom, the pyramid was their testament to history, the symbol of their reign, built to last until the end of the world; thus, the task of designing the king's burial place took precedence over virtually every other activity.

The architect Imhotep, who lived during the Third Dynasty, was the first Egyptian to design and build a pyramid. Imhotep extended the base of the mastaba (Arabic for "bench") designed for his king, Djoser, and then built six further stages, or steps, above

the mastaba in the shape of a pyramid, which rose to a height of 204 feet.

This step pyramid, located near the modern town of Saqqara, is the oldest stone building in the world. In building it Imhotep set an example for future generations of architects in Egypt who, commanded by their kings, attempted to outdo Imhotep's creation by building ever higher pyramids that symbolically bridged the gap between the earth and the heavens. To raise these stone mountains, workers quarried the blocks, which weighed as much as forty tons each, at sites as far away as Aswan, several hundred miles to the south in Upper Egypt. The stone was brought to the western bank of the river at the time of the annual flood, when the river overflowed its banks and could bring the boats as close as possible to the construction site. From the unloading platforms, the blocks were moved to the site on wooden sleds, then heaved into position along a series of ramps that were made wide and shallow at the bottom and gradually steeper as the workers moved toward the top. The pyramid was then finished with a layer of limestone quarried at Tura, on the eastern bank of the Nile.

The Old Kingdom saw the first and the last of the great pyramids, built as final resting places safe for all eternity. Later kings knew that in times of trouble, such tombs would not be secure. For example, rather than building pyramids or other imposing funerary monuments, the kings of the Eighteenth Dynasty ordered their tombs prepared in the Valley of the Kings, on the western fringe of the Nile valley near Thebes. Their purpose was secrecy, as explained by Barbara Mertz:

> The kings of the Eighteenth Dynasty got the point their ancestors had been so obtuse about—the failure of massive monuments to fulfill their major function, the protection of the royal body. The most logical conclusion would have been the practicality of a humble burial, without the gold and rich oils that tempted the poor tomb robbers. But royal majesty and human pride could not face such a conclusion. Instead, the kings strove to attain safety through secrecy. From this time on the royal tombs were all rock cut. Dug into the cliffs of a remote valley on the west bank of Thebes, their entrances were hidden, unmarked by monuments or temple.[35]

Working Stone in Ancient Egypt

While the king was still alive, the pyramids and the temples that were dedicated to their use were decorated by armies of sculptors and stonemasons. Egyptian stone carvers were experts at their craft who knew how to cut and shape limestone, diorite, basalt, dolerite, quartzite, sandstone, alabaster, and the many other varieties of stone that were quarried in Egypt and the surrounding desert.

Workers quarried the stone by chipping at it with copper chisels or hard balls of diorite (the Egyptians also used copper saws and mallets to work their stone). Sculptors and their assistants worked softer stone with chisels and saws, following a pattern that had been outlined in chalk on the stone by the master carver. The rock could be split by placing wooden wedges into the cracks, then swelling the wedges with water, or by setting fires within the cracks and then throwing cold water onto the stone (the sudden change in temperature caused the stone to split). Workers roughly shaped the stone to the desired dimensions at the quarry, then placed it on sledges, which were pushed and pulled across wooden rollers to transport vessels on the Nile.

Stone quarried in this way was used for statues of the king, for stelae (large, freestanding stones) that celebrated his accomplishments, and for reliefs of humans and the gods carved into the walls of palaces, temples, and burial chambers. Egyptian stone carvers were versatile, creating enormous statuary more than one hundred feet high as well as small figurines known as *ushabti* that were placed within the tomb before it was sealed. (The *ushabti* represented laborers who would be assigned to carry out certain tasks in the afterlife and give the tomb dweller more free time to enjoy the paradise attained after death.)

Like other artisans, stonemasons might work for nobles and even commoners who could afford their services. Their patrons had statues of themselves and of the gods created to decorate their own, much smaller and more humble tombs. They might also order freestanding sculptures for their homes or gardens. Since stone was a much more common resource than wood in ancient Egypt, sculpture served in place of furniture as the prized ornament of Egyptian homes.

The Artisan at Home

Most Egyptian artisans enjoyed a more secure and luxurious life than the peasants who worked the land. Because their skills were in

Egyptian stone carvers were capable of creating enormous statuary, such as the figures shown here at the mortuary temple built by Ramses II at Karnak.

demand by the wealthiest and most powerful members of society, their livelihoods were not dependent on the whims of landowners or the flooding of the Nile. A typical artisan's house had two, three, or four rooms, which included an entrance hall, sleeping quarters, and a back room that led out into a small garden or terrace behind the house. The flat rooftops served as a storage space or extra sleeping area on hot nights; some Egyptian homes may also have had a second story with a small terrace or balcony looking over the street. Storage cellars have also been found in Egyptian homes; in the yard were small granaries to hold the family's grain.

In the cities and among the middle classes, every home also had a "woman's quarters." Here the mothers and daughters of the household passed their time. The youngest children were cared for, and other domestic duties, such as washing and food preparation, were carried out.

Even in large homes, furnishings could be sparse. Benches for sleeping and niches for sitting were built along the walls. There were small wooden or stone stools and wooden tables for those who could afford them. Wealthier homes boasted wooden beds and mattresses, as well as rooms for washing or dining and a toilet. Windows, a high-status item, were set high in the walls to prevent the unrelenting sun from overheating the house.

Egyptian homes commonly also held a small altar or shrine, often set into the niche of a wall, at which the family honored the image of a familiar household god. Small female fertility figures have been found in the ruins of ancient Egyptian homes; these statues were believed to bring about a hoped-for pregnancy or a safe childbirth. The most popular household gods were Bes, an ugly dwarf who watched over marriage and the home, and Taweret, a pregnant hippo who protected women in the hard task of bearing and raising children.

Forerunners of the Pyramid

The pyramid developed out of earlier methods of burial that had their origins in prehistoric Egypt. Before Menes and the First Dynasty, the people of Egypt used pit burials, in which the body was placed in a shallow oval or rectangular grave and buried along with personal possessions such as weapons or pottery. During the early dynasties of the Old Kingdom, important people raised structures over their graves to preserve them from the elements and to protect the grave goods placed within from robbers. These superstructures were built out of bricks of Nile mud that were shaped and dried in the hot sun. They were built on the western bank of the Nile, because the Egyptians believed that the setting sun pointed the way to the afterlife.

These tomb structures eventually developed into the mastaba, a rectangular building raised over an underground tomb. The halls and chapels of the mastaba were open to visitors and funerary priests, while the tomb itself was sealed underground. The walls of the mastaba were brightly painted, in imitation of Egyptian homes. Reliefs were carved into the walls of the tombs, showing the deceased carrying on activities of everyday life: hunting wild animals, presiding at a feast, or offering sacrifices to the gods. Paintings showed the deceased as a figure of authority, making offerings in the role of high priest and being presented with gifts and tribute from those whom he employs and whose land he owns.

Originally protected by simple rectangular structures, pharaohs' tombs eventually came to be covered by pyramids such as these immense stone mountains at Giza.

The Secret Chambers of the Great Pyramid

Over the nearly five thousand years since it was built, there have been many explorations of the Great Pyramid of Cheops on the plain of Giza. Tomb robbers, archaeologists, and curious visitors have scrambled into the hot and nearly suffocating galleries in search of artifacts, mummies, and hidden chambers. The fact that the king's body has not been found, and that his burial chamber was found completely bare except for a sarcophagus, contributes to the speculation, and scientists are still debating the possibility of further, "secret" rooms that might lie somewhere within the structure. Michael Rice, in his book *Egypt's Making: The Origins of Ancient Egypt,* reports,

"But there always remains that most tantalizing of archaeological possibilities, the off chance that somewhere, deep inside the pyramid or far below its lowest masonry course, its principal inhabitant still lies in secret, surrounded by the treasure of a King of Egypt in his last great ceremony, his gold masked face smiling with the rictus of death and the satisfaction of having outsmarted posterity; it is an intriguing vision. Over the years during which scientific excavation has been conducted in Egypt there have occasionally been hints that 'hidden chambers' may survive in some of the pyramids. Curious noises, sudden rushes of air, or the disappearance of rainwater during a storm have all contributed to the idea that somewhere a chamber may be hidden in which an intact burial might still survive. It is, to say the least, unlikely, but it would be unwise to deny the possibility entirely."

John Romer's book *Ancient Lives: Daily Life in the Egypt of the Pharaohs* describes the house of Ramose, an artisan who lived in Deir el-Medinah, a community of laborers who lived on the western bank of the Nile near Thebes. Deir el-Medinah was home to artisans who worked on the royal tombs in the Valley of the Kings area:

Though modest by modern standards, about the same size as a small terraced house of the last century, Ramose's village house probably held larger rooms than any he had lived in before. All the village houses were of a more regular, more compact design than the usual dwellings in Thebes and many of them had ovens and cellars, cut from the desert rock. Dark, but with whitewashed walls reflecting the sunlight which fell from small slots in the roof, their public rooms held cushioned couches, neat wooden chairs and cabinets of rush and wood, containing a little stela with a prayer carved on it and with busts, perhaps, of the ancestors standing close by. The largest room was probably reserved for gatherings of friends, for there was no square, no open ground, near the village where people could meet in the evenings. So we may imagine villagers seated in a parlor, bright beams of light holding in them the smoke from the ovens and dust hovering in the air. The white wooden door is open to the street, old friends make music together, play games or simply sit and talk, and children run in and out and all around.[36]

A Lifetime Spent
Preparing for Death

Religious belief formed a vital part of daily life for the ancient Egyptians, whose gods took on vivid human or animal form in art, architecture, and writing. Religious belief was held in a very personal way as well. Each man and woman carried on a certain relationship with the gods he or she believed in, addressing his or her prayers and supplications to the deities that watched over life, work, home, and family. All Egyptians hoped for the favor of the gods that would bring good fortune, and all feared the wrath of those gods who demanded attention and sacrifice from all who would remain in their good graces.

In ancient Egypt, there was no doubt about the existence of the gods and their powers. The effects of the supernatural were present everywhere: in the rising of the sun or moon; in the annual rising of a bright star, Sirius, which brought the flood in early summer; in the growth of new crops each year; and in the bounty of the fields, rivers, hills, and desert. Together and side by side, the immortal gods and mortal humans carried on a never-ending companionship.

Creation

In Egyptian belief, the world was formed out of the cold and chaotic, watery land of Nun. From this somber region, a mound of earth slowly emerged; a temple arose at the summit of the mound. The temple separated the gods above from the world below and contained a shelter to mark the sacred spot of the world's origin.

At the creation, all of the gods and the human race emerged, fully formed and in a state of perfection, along with all of the principles and ideals on which the world was founded: law, religion, royalty, writing, and art. In ancient Egypt, the quest of the artist, architect, and sculptor was to imitate and realize the conditions that were present at the creation. According to scholar A. Rosalie David,

> In this belief, they differed widely from ourselves, who accept the idea of a constantly changing society with new sets of values, new solutions to fresh problems, and advances in many aspects of learning. It is not surprising that the Egyptians should cling to such beliefs, for their surroundings—the yearly renewal of the seasons which is so apparent in Egypt—must have suggested to them that life was a cyclical process, whose pattern had been established at some far distant date and which would never change.[37]

Behind all religious practice and belief lay the promise of the afterlife, when the man or woman living a righteous life joined the gods in their lush and happy paradise.

Death

Among the ancient Egyptians, the preparation for death and burial was one of life's most important activities. During their lifetimes, the kings of Egypt had armies of laborers and artisans hard at work on their royal tombs, which could take decades to complete. The erection of mastaba tombs and pyramids began in the early dynasties of the Old Kingdom. These monuments sheltered the remains of the dead pharaohs, and spells were inscribed on the walls of the tomb to ensure the occupant's safe and certain passage to the paradise of the afterlife. Ordinary Egyptians, however, could only hope for a decent burial in a protected place that might shelter them from wild animals and grave robbers.

During the Middle Kingdom, Egyptian beliefs underwent an important transformation, and as a result the afterlife became a more democratic place. The Old Kingdom sun god, Re, went out of fashion, while Osiris, traditionally worshiped as the god of the dead, took preeminence. According to legend, Osiris was a human who was murdered by his evil brother, Seth. After his death, Osiris was resurrected to become the king of the underworld. Egyptians came to believe that ordinary people, as well as kings, could take the journey to the afterlife. If properly prepared and carried out, funeral preparations and rites would allow eternal life among the gods in the underworld, the realm presided over by Osiris. According to one account, when a human died,

The Egyptians . . . envisioned a divine committee judging souls before allowing them entry into Duat, the land of the justified dead. Anubis, protector of mum-

The god Osiris was believed to have been a human murdered by his evil brother and resurrected as king of the underworld.

mies, placed the heart of the deceased on scales and weighed it against a feather worn in the headdress of Maat, goddess of order. Thoth, wise and honest scribe of the gods, recorded the good and bad the heart contained. Those whose hearts balanced perfectly with the feather won eternal life; the rejected were devoured by Ammit, monster of the dead.[38]

According to Egyptian belief, the tomb was the realm of the *ka*, or spiritual double, which served as an individual's conscience during his or her life and as the everlasting soul or essence after death. The *ka* was served by the offerings and possessions brought to the tomb by members of the family or by specially appointed "*ka* priests." Another part of the soul, the *ba*, was the spirit that escaped after death to travel freely, representing the last link to the land of living mortals. The *ba* was depicted in Egyptian paintings as a bird with a human head that could fly out of the body. According to historian John A. Wilson, "The ba or 'soul' was that element of a man's personality which had effective play after death, particularly in maintaining contact between the man's akh or 'effective being' in another world and his corpse, tomb, and survivors in this world."[39] Many Egyptians believed that the *ba* could also leave the body while they were still alive and that their dreams represented the free-ranging flight of the *ba*.

There was one more important aspect to life and death—the *akh*. The Egyptians believed that the body itself was transformed into the *akh*, the form in which it survived after death. In order for a proper transformation, however, all the essential ingredients of the living individual had to be preserved, through spells, incantations, prayer, and the right actions of family survivors and priests after the funeral ceremony took place.

The Egyptian god Anubis, generally depicted with the head of a jackal, was believed to be the protector of mummies.

The Egyptians equipped their tombs to provide for life after death, providing all the food, household goods, and personal possessions considered necessary in the afterlife. Small models of the departed's home would provide shelter; weapons interred with the body would allow a hunter to pursue his sport. Tomb paintings showed the activities that would be carried out after death—hunting, feasting, and the like—as well as servants and peasants carrying out their normal duties of providing for their dead masters.

According to Egyptian belief, these scenes and figures would be magically brought to life by a ceremony performed during the funeral rites. To avoid necessary work that the dead might be called on to perform in the afterlife, *ushabti* statuettes were placed in the tomb to serve as substitutes. Christine Hobson writes,

> To counteract . . . eternal servitude, in the Middle Kingdom, for the first time tiny worker figures were provided to "answer" when the god summoned the soul. Since the Egyptian for "answer" is "usheb," the figures are called "ushabtis." In later times, in a perfectly equipped tomb there would be 401 ushabtis: 365, one for every day of the year, and 36 overseers, one for every 10 workers! The front of the ushabti was either inscribed simply with the deceased's name or, often, with a spell to make it work: "O Ushabti, if I am summoned or assessed to do any work which is to be done in the land of the dead—if problems are piled up for me by (any) man concerning his (own) work in sowing fields, irrigating the arable land or in shipping stone from east bank to west bank, say—I shall do it! I am here! You shall answer to it!"[40]

The Book of the Dead

The ancient Egyptians created thousands of hymns, prayers, and formulas for the purpose of preparing the soul of the dead—the *ka*—for the journey to the afterlife. Committing these texts to memory while still alive, and having them sung or chanted during the funeral ceremony, allowed the *ka* to avoid harm from the evil spirits lying in wait after death.

The Egyptians began recording their funerary texts during the Old Kingdom, when scribes rendered them in hieroglyphics and stonemasons cut them into the walls of the royal pyramids. Later, during the Middle Kingdom, ordinary citizens had the texts painted on their stone coffins. Scribes also wrote them on papyri scrolls that were then placed within the wrappings of mummies. By the time of the New Kingdom, about two hundred spells and prayers had been collected into the Book of the Dead, a work that would be left inside the tombs to help the deceased. One of the chapters of the Book of the Dead was intended to help the dead pass judgment in the next world, which was known as Amentit. One author notes,

> The whole of the one hundred and twenty-fifth chapter of the Book of the Dead was written in order to shrive the sinner of his sins. The Egyptians sometimes copied it onto a roll of papyrus which was then laid in the coffin between the mummy's legs. It reads like an eyewitness account of the last judgment—written in anticipation of the event—but this is a judgment where everything works out for the best.[41]

Making Mummies

The preservation of the physical body after death was very important to the ancient Egyptians, since they believed that the continued life of the *ka* depended on the continued existence of its former home. They carried out this preservation through the art and science of mummification.

The making of mummies may have begun when the early Egyptians noticed that the dry desert sands naturally preserved dead bodies. Eventually, mummy making became a highly specialized profession in ancient Egypt. The Egyptians refined mummification into a process so effective that the bodies of hundreds of ancient Egyptian pharaohs, nobles, and commoners survive nearly intact down to the present day.

Mummification was a process that could take a few days, in the case of a commoner, to two months or longer, in the case of an Egyptian king. To prepare the body, the organs and brains were removed, set in a compound of preserving salts, and placed in canopic jars that would also be placed within the tomb. However, the heart, which was considered the seat of wisdom and of the soul, was left inside the body. The body was then placed in natron, a mineral salt that dried it out, and then washed and wrapped in thick layers of linen cloth. The dried-out body was sometimes filled out with sawdust or linen to prevent it from shrinking.

Between the linen wrapping, the embalmers laid amulets and tokens to protect the corpse from attack and thievery. At the end, a ceremony known as "The Opening of the Mouth" was performed to restore life to the mummy and send it on its way. For the protection of the preserved bodies of the deceased, the Egyptians inscribed terrible curses on the outside of the tombs, threatening

A Reading from the Book of the Dead

Modern Egyptologists give the title Book of the Dead to several collections of funerary texts. One of these texts, titled "The Chapter of Coming Forth by Day and of Opening Up a Way Through the Amehet," which appears on a website maintained by the Egyptian Tourism Ministry, describes the efforts of the soul to pass judgment and reach the promised paradise.

"Behold, the scribe Nebseni, whose word is truth, saith: Homage to you, O ye Lords of Kau, ye who are without sin, and who live for the endless and infinite aeons of time which make up eternity. I have opened up a way for myself to you. I have become a spirit in my forms, I have gotten the mastery over my words of magical power, and I am adjudged a spirit; therefore deliver ye me from the Crocodile [which liveth in] this Country of Truth. Grant ye to me my mouth that I may speak therewith, and cause ye that sepulchral offerings shall be made unto me in your presence, for I know you, and I know your names, and I know also the name of the mighty god before whose face ye set your celestial food. His name is 'Tekem.'

[When] he openeth up his path on the eastern horizon of heaven, [when] he alighteth towards the western horizon of heaven, may he carry me along with him, and may I be safe and sound. Let not the Mesqet make an end of me, let not the Fiend (Sebau) gain the mastery over me, let me not be driven away from the doors of the Other World, let not your doors be shut in my face, for my cakes are in the city of Pe, and my ale is in the city of Tep. And there, in the celestial mansions of heaven which my divine father Tem hath established, let my hands lay hold upon the wheat and the barley, which shall be given unto me therein in abundant measure, and may the son of my own body make ready for me my food therein. And grant ye unto me when I am there sepulchral meals, and incense, and unguents, and all the pure and beautiful things whereon the god liveth, in every deed for ever, in all the transformations which it pleaseth me [to perform], and grant unto me the power to float down and to sail up the stream in the Field of Reeds (Sekhet-Aaru), [and may I reach Sekhet-hetepet (the Field of Offerings)]. I am the twin Lion-gods (Shu and Tefnut)."

This artist's rendering depicts the process of mummification, which took anywhere from a few days to a few months, depending on the social class of the deceased.

a violent death to raiders or robbers and a very severe judgment in the afterworld. One such curse from a tomb at Saqqara reads,

> As for anything that you might do against this tomb of mine of the West, the like shall be done against your property. I am an excellent lector priest, exceedingly knowledgeable in secret spells and all magic. As for any person who will enter into this tomb of mine in their impurity . . . I shall seize him like a goose, placing fear in him at seeing ghosts upon earth. . . . But as for anyone who will enter into this tomb of mine being pure and peaceful regarding it, I shall be his protective backer in the West in the court of the great god.[42]

In ancient Egypt, the care of the dead did not end with a funeral ceremony. A funerary cult served the deceased in the years after his or her death. Services were performed and offerings made in the tomb's chapel, which remained open to visitors from the outside world. The living arrived regularly to pronounce the names of the offering bearers painted on the walls of the tomb, an action believed to bring these figures to life and continue to serve the dead after the living had departed. *Ka* priests were hired by those who could afford them to carry on the funerary cult. For the king of Egypt, an entire temple might be built and hundreds of priests and others employed to sustain the funerary cult.

Living with the Gods

The Egyptians worshiped their gods in many forms. At one time, every town and village up and down the Nile River had a particular local deity, which would be unknown to people living elsewhere in the country. By the time of the Old Kingdom, Egypt was home to many cults devoted to the worship of cows, crocodiles, cats, snakes, and other creatures present in the daily world. Anthropomorphic local gods, who took on human form in paintings or statuary, were honored in certain regions or cities, where the people raised temples to them and carried out annual or seasonal rites in their honor. In many regions, a triad of closely related gods existed to which the local people made regular offerings. In the region of Aswan, in distant Upper Egypt, for example, the ram-headed Khnum reigned with his two consorts, Satis and Anukis.

Other cults were devoted to individual deities. Sobek, the crocodile god, was worshiped at a place called Crocodilopolis, in the Faiyum region west of the Nile in Lower Egypt. The priests of Sobek had to take certain

The crocodile god Sobek, shown here with Isis, was unknown in most of Egypt, but was worshipped in Crocodilopolis.

risks to carry out these rites, as described by the ancient Greek writer Strabo, who once witnessed the ceremony:

> It [Sobek] is fed with the bread, meat, and wine brought by the strangers who come to see it. Our host went with us to the lake, taking along a small meal-cake, some meat, and a small flask of wine. We found the animal lying on the bank; the priests approached and, while some of them opened his jaws, another thrust first the cake into his mouth, then the meat, and finally poured the wine after them. Thereupon the crocodile plunged into the lake and swam to the opposite shore.[43]

The ancient Egyptians worshiped several more-important gods whose cult extended throughout the kingdom. Sekhmet, the goddess of the desert and of warfare, possessed a human body and the head of a lion. Ptah was the god of artisans and the god of crafts, building, and the workshop. Anubis, a god represented with the head of a jackal, presided over mummification and the preparation of the dead for the underworld. He was believed to live in the mountains of the west, the final destination of the dead. Thoth, a wise god shown as an ibis or as a baboon, watched over the scribes, who invoked his help and protection while undertaking their demanding profession. Khnum was a god of pottery, while Hathor was the goddess of music, art, and dancing.

The National Gods

Certain deities rose to the rank of a "national" god, recognized and worshiped by all Egyptians. This sometimes happened when a powerful pharaoh imposed the god of his native region on the entire kingdom. The first of these was Re, a sun god whose representative on earth was the king. According to writer James Henry Breasted, Egypt's weather had much to do with the rise of Re:

> In a land where a clear sky prevailed and rain was rarely seen the incessant splendour of the sun was an insistent fact, which gave him the highest place in the thought and daily life of the people. His worship was almost universal, but the chief centre of his cult was at On, the Delta city, which the Greeks called Heliopolis. Here he was known as Re, which was the solar orb itself; or as Atum, the name of the decrepit sun, as an old man tottering down the west; again his name Khepri, written with a beetle in hieroglyphics, designated him in the youthful vigour of his rising.[44]

The Egyptians made Heliopolis into an astronomical observatory as well as a religious center. Here the priests of the sun god Re studied the movement of the heavenly bodies in the sky and the measurement of time and years.

After the First Intermediate Period, the worship of Re declined as the sun god was replaced by Osiris, the god of the dead and the underworld. Osiris won favor among the common Egyptians through his mythical triumph over adversity and his attainment of immortality. The Osiris myth held out the promise of everlasting life to all people, no matter their social rank or wealth. The cult also gave rise to a pilgrimage, aspired to by every Egyptian once during his or her lifetime, to cult centers at Abydos and Busiris.

The New Kingdom saw the rise of a new national god, a successor to Osiris known as Amon-Re, which combined aspects of Re and Amon (or Amen), the local god of Thebes. The worship of Amon-Re rose along with the powerful and wealthy New Kingdom rulers who came from that region. Immense temples were

One Egyptian king attempted to carry out a religious revolution. This was Akhenaton, originally known as Amenophis IV, who ruled at the end of the Eighteenth Dynasty. After attaining the throne of Egypt, Akhenaton banished the state gods, including the powerful Amon-Re. He banned their worship and had their statues, paintings, reliefs, and other depictions defaced or destroyed. He turned Egypt into a monotheistic society that worshiped one god: Aten, depicted not in human or animal form but as the disk of the sun. In reliefs showing the god, Aten sent out its rays in the form of outstretched human hands to worshipers on earth.

By abandoning Amon-Re and the rest of Egypt's deities, Akhenaton made a drastic break with the kings and the beliefs of the past. He also abandoned the old capitals of Egypt and built an entirely new city, Akhetaten, on a strip of empty land halfway between Thebes and Memphis. The city was laid out with broad streets and spacious public squares. Lavish palaces were built for Akhenaton and his royal officials. On boundary markers placed around the new city, Akhenaton proudly proclaimed, as cited in Dietrich Wildung's *Egypt: From Prehistory to the Romans*,

"The Aten, my father, it was that pointed to Akhetaten. Look, the pharaoh found it! No god, no goddess, no ruler, no official and no person can lay claim to it. I erect Akhetaten for the Aten, my father, at this place. I build the great temple for the Aten, my father, in Akhetaten in this place. And I build the small temple for the Aten, my father, in Akhetaten in this place. . . . I build for myself palaces for the pharaoh, and I build a harem for the royal consort in Akhetaten in this place. I have a tomb built in the mountain of Akhetaten, where the sun rises, where I shall be buried after the millions of years' reign."

Rather than millions of years, however, Akhenaton's reign lasted only about fifteen. Upon Akhenaton's death, and young Tutankhamen's accession, Tell el-Amarna was abandoned, the worship of Aten ended, and the old gods regained their places. Tutankhamen had his laborers and artisans deface the king's images, destroy his temples to the disk of the sun, and erase his name wherever they found it. In this way, Tutankhamen banished Akhenaton's strange monotheistic religion, as well as his memory, for all time—or so the king believed.

This sandstone bust depicts Akhenaton, an Egyptian king who attempted to replace the worship of Egypt's many gods with that of a single god, Aten.

raised to the god at Karnak and at nearby Thebes. The rise of Amon-Re made the god's priesthood so powerful and wealthy that it rivaled the power of the kings themselves. According to one account, these priests

> had enjoyed unparalleled prestige and power. Throughout the 18th Dynasty, their temples to Amen had dominated the economic life of the realm. Tithes and tributes flowed into Amen's treasuries, and the god's granaries held the nation's surplus grain. The Amen priesthood sent its own trading missions to foreign parts and controlled the labor forces for public works at home.[45]

Throughout ancient times, Egyptians of all classes and ranks sought to identify themselves closely with these powerful national deities. The nobles and landowners aspired to a place of their own in the most prestigious temples by offering land or an annual tribute. Good works such as these might be rewarded with a statue of themselves that would be raised in the temple forecourt, and to which food and drink would be offered by devoted priests or descendants as long as the temple stood.

Ordinary citizens could never wander very deep inside these imposing temples, where images and statues of the Egyptian gods were kept in the deepest, most closely guarded sanctuary. In this chamber, only the high priest and the king himself were allowed to enter. But citizens could have their prayers and supplications written down by a scribe and carried into the temple. Once a year, during the god's festival, they also had a chance to view the god. The sacred image was carried out of the local temple and placed on top of a gilded wooden boat. The residents gathered along the streets to watch the procession of priests carry the god's image. Those who wished could pose questions to the god, in the form of two opposing statements inscribed on shards of pottery. While making the rounds of the city, the image of the god would be seen to nod to one of the shards, in this way providing an answer to the query. Gradually, the priests and citizens wound their way back through the streets and alleys and finally to the temple, the god's permanent home.

Temples of the Gods and Man

For the Egyptians, the earthly home of the gods was a building set completely apart from the everyday world. It was, according to the British writer Lord Kinross,

> a holy city within a city, endowed with its own lands and revenues, as a monastery is, inhabited by a large staff of priests, scribes, overseers, managers, civil servants, artisans, craftsmen, and other employees of the god. . . . Unlike the Christian church or the Greek temple, it was a sanctuary for the god and his hierarchy of priests, rather than for the people, who did not worship him publicly and were excluded from the rites in his holy of holies.[46]

There were two kinds of temples in ancient Egypt. The "cultus" temple, dedicated to a god, was built to house an image of the god and for the purpose of honoring that image with ceremonies and offerings. The Egyptians built "mortuary" temples to commemorate a worldly ruler and to celebrate his achievements after his death. Because the temples represented eternal aspects of the gods and the semidivine kings, they were built of an everlasting material—stone.

Whatever their purpose, all Egyptian temples were designed with certain common features. In front of the temple was a great doorway, known as a pylon, which consisted of two sloping walls rising on either side of a massive doorway. Beyond the doorway was an open court, which might contain statues of the gods or kings as well as reliefs carved into the walls and columns. Beyond the court was a hypostyle hall, an enclosed room in which the roof was supported by rows of carved and painted columns.

The temple halls were filled with statuary and stelae, small stone monuments carrying pictures and/or inscriptions. Some wall inscriptions record important events, sacred rit-uals, and prayers, as well as the triumphs of the king who had them built. In surviving hypostyle halls, the great mass of pillars rising to a high ceiling gives the impression of a great stone forest—an imitation of the forest the Egyptians believed to grow in the paradise of the afterworld. For example, the hypostyle hall of the mortuary temple built by Ramses II at Karnak, the largest hall of columns in the world, covers fifty-four thousand square feet, and its intricately carved and painted pillars tower sixty-nine feet.

The *naos,* or innermost sanctuary of the temple, lay at the far end of the hypostyle

The hypostyle halls of temples contained a mass of pillars meant to symbolize the forest that Egyptians believed to grow in the afterworld.

hall. Here the sacred images were kept, and nobody but the king and the high priest of the temple, as the deputy of the king, could enter. It was these priests' obligation to carry out a prescribed ritual each morning within the sanctuary. They purified the room, performed a chant to honor the god, and made offerings of food, drink, and incense to the god's image. The priests also presided at festivals, during which processions made their way through the streets to arrive at the temple itself, stopping before reaching the sanctuary. These festivals might celebrate the annual flood of the Nile, the coronation of a king, an important battle victory, or the legendary events in the myth of the god or goddess. The occasion was always memorable for the common people, as Barbara Mertz explains:

> In all this elaborate [religious] activity the common people had little or no part. The only time they saw the god, or his gorgeous golden shrine, was when he went traveling on the occasion of some festival. Luckily for the Egyptian laboring man there were many festivals; at some periods almost one-third of the days were holy days.[47]

The temples of ancient Egypt were important economic centers as well as religious shrines. The wealthiest temples owned great estates of land, buildings, and cities, and were paid regular tributes of grain and other goods. They employed thousands of workers, priests, and officials, many of whom handed down their positions to their sons. The most prosperous temple estate of ancient Egypt, that of Amon-Re at Karnak, owned more than a half million acres of land and more than fifty cities and towns. For many years, the high priests of Amon-Re rivaled their own kings in wealth and influence over the affairs of the state.

Leisure Time in Ancient Egypt

For the ancient Egyptians, each day of the year had a certain significance. There were good and bad days for farming, for travel, for religious ritual, for warfare, and for leisure pursuits such as feasting, hunting, and fishing. According to the Cairo Calendar, an artifact that provides information about Egyptian astrology, certain mythological events were associated with each day, and certain activities and behavior were appropriate on particular days.

Festivals

The Egyptians celebrated the most important days of the year with a festival. The New Year (*sopdit*) was celebrated when the Nile River began to rise, a time that coincided each year with the rising of the star Sirius and which was marked by the giving of offerings to the gods by both city dwellers and villagers. During the inundation, the festival of *opet* was celebrated with the procession of a sacred boat of the god Amon, which proceeded along the Nile River to the cheers and admiration of the people along the riverbanks. Bastet, a god representing passion and maternal love that appeared in the form of a cat, was worshiped in and around the city of Bubastis. The Greek traveler and historian Herodotus described the annual festivals at Bubastis:

The procedure at Bubastis is this: they come in barges, men and women together, a great number in each boat; on the way, some of the women keep up a continual clatter with castanets and some of the men play flutes, while the rest, both men and women, sing and clap their hands. Whenever they pass a town on the river-bank, they bring the barge close inshore, some of the women continuing to act as I have said, while others shout abuse at the women of the place, or start dancing, or stand up and hitch up their skirts. When they reach Bubastis they celebrate the festival with elaborate sacrifices, and more wine is consumed than during all the rest of the year.[48]

Small towns and villages celebrated their local gods and also honored the great national gods on certain days. On these occasions, work was suspended, offerings were made, and the streets were filled with revellers. Little or no work was carried out on the first day of each *decan* (the Egyptian week, made up of ten days). There were also evil days on which one had to proceed with great caution, as recounted by Pierre Montet:

The birthday of Set . . . was hostile, and the whole day was spent by the kings in complete idleness and neglect even of their own persons. Private individuals also adjusted their behaviour to the character of the days. . . . Prohibited activities might include bathing, embarking in a boat, making a journey, eating fish or anything which lived in water, or killing a goat, an ox, or a duck.[49]

At the Banquet

During a local festival, or on special occasions such as a religious ceremony, Egyptians celebrated among neighbors and family with a feast of eating, drinking, music, and dancing. Landowners and the aristocracy prepared an evening banquet, an occasion for both men and women to put on their finery and make an attractive display of themselves. Men and women wore their finest clothes woven from Egypt's abundant flax (animal skins and wool were considered impure and were shunned as clothing material in ancient Egypt). Hair was carefully cut, groomed with fine-toothed combs of bone or wood, and conditioned with beeswax and fragrant lotions. Men or women might also wear wigs—short and curly hair for men, longer and flowing for women, some-

times piled on top of their heads like a beehive. It was common practice for women to place a cake made of a combination of wax and perfume atop their heads before attending a banquet; as the festivities continued, the perfume would gradually melt and flow down around their heads and necks, lending a strong and pleasant scent to the air surrounding them.

Once seated, the guests had the opportunity to sample the best food and delicacies the household could offer. They used bowls, cups, plates, and goblets fashioned from rock crystal, schist, alabaster, gold, or silver. The banquet featured the roast meat of domestic cattle or pigs, or wild game captured in the desert or the valley. The meat was cooked in oil, spiced with garlic, fennel, cumin, thyme, or dill, and sweetened with honey or dates. Pigeons, ducks, geese, and other fowl were also dressed and roasted on a spit. Sweet breads and fruits decorated the table, where guests helped themselves from large dishes and ate with their fingers. Wine—an expensive luxury item—was

This relief found on the tomb of Ramose depicts a man wearing a wig, a common practice in ancient Egypt.

The ancient Egyptians of all classes, and both sexes, used cosmetics and perfume and wore jewelry. Women painted their lips and fingernails and used dark paint to outline and enhance their eyes. Green eye paint, or malachite, was made from copper, while black eye paint, known as kohl, was made from soot, from crushed galena rock, or from lead. Henna, a reddish dye, could be spread on the nails, palms, feet, and hair. Perfumes made from incense or myrrh were mixed into an oil base and spread over the skin.

Jewelry adorned the plain linen clothing of the ancient Egyptians. Both men and women wore earrings, bracelets, necklaces, and rings. The jewelry was made of strings of colored beads or from semiprecious stones such as garnet, onyx, or amethyst. Lapis lazuli was a favorite jewelry material. The Egyptians also wore amulets, such as the eye of the falcon god Horus, in the belief that these would guard them against illness or injury.

Besides their wealth of jewelry and personal adornment, the Egyptians were renowned throughout the ancient world for the great care they took of their bodies. Barbers, manicurists, and chiropodists (who took care of the feet) were busily occupied in the streets and in the homes of the wealthy. To keep their bodies fresh, the Egyptians used a compound of turpentine and incense; they also used lotions for the skin, deodorants, wrinkle creams, and hair and scalp conditioners.

This wooden box holds bottles that contained cosmetics and perfumes popular in ancient Egypt. Great care was taken in physical appearance and cleanliness.

Leisure Time in Ancient Egypt **69**

This wall painting depicts a harpist singing and playing for Anhour Khaou, the chief builder of Thebes, and his wife.

prepared in the Faiyum area or in certain parts of the Delta where the soil and climate were suitable for grapes.

To entertain the guests, musicians and dancers were hired. Starting in the Middle Kingdom, at the rise of Osiris and his myth, dance became an important part of rituals and festivals. Dancers performed carefully choreographed movements during the festivals associated with Osiris and his sister/wife, Isis. The website "The Magic and Mysteries of Ancient Egypt" further describes Egyptian dancing:

> Dance figured, too, in private life. Professional performers entertained at social

events, and traveling troupes gave performances in public squares of great cities such as Thebes and Alexandria. Movements of Egyptian dances were named after the motion they imitated. For instance, there were "the leading along of an animal," "the taking of gold," and "the successful capture of the boat."[50]

Egyptian music was performed on harps, lyres, and flutes made of reed stalks. Small drums made of wood and animal skins accompanied the music and provided rhythm for dancers. The Egyptians also made small hand clappers for dancers and for everyday use, when music sung and chanted provided rhythm and relief from the drudgery of work or farming. During the New Kingdom, the Egyptians began forming larger groups of a dozen or more musicians.

Nobody can say for certain what the music of ancient Egypt sounded like. Although music formed a part of religious ritual as well as everyday life and leisure, the ancient Egyptians did not have a system of notating the music that they performed. As a result, no authentic ancient Egyptian music has survived to the present day. Musicians learned their music by rote or played spontaneously.

The feast of a king or noble might also include a special attraction for the guests: the appearance of native-born dwarves (*nmiu*) or pygmies (*dng*), who were imported into the country from central Africa. Both dwarves and pygmies were reputed to be fine dancers, and they were highly prized entertainers at the royal courts of Egypt. They were also used in ceremonies by the priests of the temples.

Hunting and Fishing

On a day of rest, or in the wet season when work in the fields was impossible, Egyptian families made excursions into the country for hunting, fishing, picnicking, and relaxation. Such day-tripping was popular among all classes, from the rural peasant up to the king himself, who might order an excursion of hundreds of servants, friends, and officials into a favored part of the valley or the Nile Delta.

The Egyptians remained avid and skilled hunters after leaving behind the nomadic lifestyle of their prehistory, when wild game had provided the mainstay of the diet. When he hunted, the Egyptian was returning to the simpler prehistoric time when, according to James Breasted,

In the unsubdued jungles of the Nile, animal life was of course much more plentiful . . . the elephant, giraffe, hippopotamus and the strange okapi [small giraffes], which was deified as the god Set, wandered through the jungles. . . . These early men were therefore great hunters, as well as skillful fishermen. They pursued the most formidable game of the desert, like the lion or the wild ox, with bows and arrows; and in light boats they attacked the hippopotamus and the crocodile with harpoons and lances.[51]

After the rise of the pharaohs and Egyptian agriculture, there was no lack of game. Gazelles, jackals, wild cats, and antelopes could be found in the "black land"—the valley of the Nile—as well as the "red land" of the nearby desert. Watering holes provided good hunting grounds, especially during the dry season when the river ran low. Hunters used spears, bows and arrows, and nets to capture wild game, while small wooden traps attracted turtles and wild hares. A favorite sport of Egyptian aristocrats was hunting with the boomerang, an expensive weapon acquired in trade from Nubia and central Africa.

To hunt the dangerous and unpredictable hippopotamuses, which gathered in small herds, the Egyptians attempted to separate one specimen from the group and then entangle it with barbed ropes or harpoon it to death. Bird hunters used nets and throwing sticks to kill their prey. A more effective way to hunt birds was to set traps, which might be simple nets laid beside a watering hole or pond baited with fish and tame birds used as lures.

For the nobles and kings of Egypt, a desert hunt provided an occasion for a display of skill, bravery, and luck—the qualities to be demonstrated in anyone presuming to lead a society. Professional guides and hunters led the party into the likeliest regions, tracking the game to its dens, rock shelters, and watering holes. Beside them roamed faithful hunting dogs, used to scent and find game. Hyenas, with their strong scent that masked the presence of humans, horses, and dogs, were sometimes used as decoys.

Once the prey was located, the dogs attacked, either driving the game into the open or attacking it directly. The hunters used lassos, spears, and bows and arrows to capture and kill the prey. Traps and nets might be used to capture smaller animals. By the time of the New Kingdom, the Hyksos had brought horses to the Nile valley, and hunting parties often rode in search of their game mounted in horse-drawn chariots.

Hunting Crocodiles

In his famous account of the manners, customs, and religion of Egypt, the Greek historian Herodotus gives the following eyewitness account of one of the most dangerous hunts of all: the hunt for the deadly Nile crocodile.

"Of the numerous different ways of catching crocodiles I will describe the one which seems to me the most interesting. They bait a hook with a chine of pork and let it float out into midstream, and at the same time, standing on the bank, take a live pig and beat it. The crocodile, hearing its squeals, makes a rush towards it, encounters the bait, gulps it down, and is hauled out of the water. The first thing the huntsman does when he has got the beast on land is to plaster its eyes with mud; this done, it is dispatched easily enough—but without this precaution it will give a lot of trouble."

Fishing

The Nile and the nearby waters of lakes and streams provided carp, mullet, catfish, eels, and other species for fishers (Egyptian civilians rarely ventured as far as the Mediterranean Sea, which to them represented the unknown and frightening edge of the world). Fishermen dropped long seines—finely meshed fishing nets—to the shallow bottoms of rivers and lakes, waited for the fish to swim above the seine, then pulled it to the surface. They also used keep nets, small wicker traps that were open at one end and closed at the other end to form a narrow neck. The keep net was baited and then left to drift through the water, where fish in search of food would swim through the larger opening. Reed stalks were placed in a way that made it impossible for the fish to escape the trap once inside.

Egyptian fishermen also used cast nets made from papyrus or reed twine. The nets were tossed into the water from shore or from a small boat, then sank under the weight of stones or lead fastened to their edges. Fishing lines tied to hooks of copper or bronze were also used. Those who could afford them used long, barbed harpoons to catch and kill their prey in the most direct manner possible. Although fishing was a favored leisure-time activity, those who practiced it had to keep a very sharp eye out for the Nile crocodiles that shared the watercourses and could easily make a quick meal of a human being.

Games and Sports

In addition to hunting, the Egyptians amused themselves with games and physical contests such as wrestling. The host of a banquet might put on an entire series of wrestling matches for the evening entertainment of his

This wall painting depicts the god Nakht using a throwing stick to hunt birds in the Nile marshes. Weapons commonly used to hunt in ancient Egypt included spears, bows and arrows, nets, and small wooden traps.

guests. Egyptian wall paintings also show boys taking part in boxing and wrestling, which served as a toughening sport for young men as well as a spectator sport. According to Guillemette Andreu,

> One boys' game known from several representations seems brutal, almost cruel: one of the adolescents was captured by a group of youths and cornered in an enclosed area. Like a mouse trapped by a cat, he had to escape from this tight spot on his own. If he succeeded, he was considered "great." The little girls did not take part in this sort of exercise; they studied dancing, practicing to take part in the festivals honoring the goddess Hathor, mistress of music, love, and dance.[52]

Many of these games and sports were not just simple recreation—they had religious significance as well. On the walls of temples and tombs, Egyptian men are shown taking part in a stick fighting game, which represented not just an earthly contest of strength but also the battle between Horus, the son of Osiris, and Seth, the evil god that killed Osiris.

Egyptian children had access to a variety of toys and games, as evidenced by the contents of tombs. In some cases, toys have been found within the coffins or burial sites of children, who were buried with small dolls made

Ancient Egyptians enjoyed various board games. This ivory game board dates from the Twelfth Dynasty.

of reeds or clay, balls made of leather and stuffed with straw, jacks, wooden tops, and game boards. Children pulled wooden horses on wheels and played with small models of cats, mice, lions, and other familiar animals. Dolls were made of wood, with strings of beads representing hair.

In their leisure time, the Egyptians enjoyed board games such as checkers. In his book *The Culture of Ancient Egypt*, John A. Wilson describes the discovery of a checkerboard that archaeologists dated to predynastic times:

Excavation has produced a crude kind of checkerboard. It is a table of unbaked clay with four stumpy legs, its surface divided into eighteen squares, and accompanied by about a dozen game pieces of clay coated with wax. Such an apparatus for amusement is significant. There must

already have been the slight surplus of wealth which relieved the pressure of endless toil; there must already have been the leisure time for entertainment.[53]

Egyptians also enjoyed the game known as *senet*. This strategy game was played on a rectangular playing board of stone or wood. Thirty squares, in three long rows of ten, were either drawn or carved on top of the board. Opponents moved their opposing sets of stones or playing pieces around the board, according to the indications of sticks thrown down on the ground. Certain hazards or lucky squares on the *senet* board helped the player with symbols of long life or magical protection. Another board game, *mehen*, was played with dice and playing pieces that were moved around a small circular table carved in the shape of a coiling snake.

Travel in Ancient Egypt

The better off an Egyptian was, the more leisure time he had. The wealthy even had time for leisurely travel to other parts of the kingdom. For long-distance transportation, the Egyptians used boats of every size and description. The Nile's current allowed a swift and easy trip downriver, to the north. To travel from the frontier of Nubia, far in the south in Upper Egypt, all the way to the Nile Delta in Lower Egypt might take only two or three weeks with the help of a strong, flood-season current. Going south, against the current, was made easy by the prevailing winds, which blew from the north.

For trips to nearby towns or hunting grounds, the wealthy Egyptians used horse-drawn chariots (the horse had arrived in Egypt with the Hyksos invasion). Before the arrival of the chariot, it was the duty of certain servants to carry the wealthy along the road in litters (carrying chairs), some of which could also be saddled to the back of a strong mule. Such trips were not undertaken lightly. The expedition of a king and his court into the desert might require the labor of hundreds of slaves to transport baggage, food, arms, and litters of nobles and officials.

Even for the wealthy, traveling in ancient Egypt could be dangerous, especially when one ventured far from towns or from the valley of the Nile into the desert. Robbers and other riffraff lived in the remote cliffs and hills, making a living from the goods they could steal from wayfarers. In the desert, wandering Bedouin or Arabs might stop a traveling caravan and demand tribute, or a trade of merchandise, before allowing travelers to continue. Soldiers, who were poorly paid but skilled with

Due to Egypt's proximity to the Nile, Egyptians used boats of various sizes to travel long distances.

arms and armor, also had the reputation of stealing clothing, food, and especially shoes and weapons from strangers on the road.

Egypt had a good network of roads, for all the earthmoving demanded by the building of canals provided plenty of raw material for road surfacing. Throughout the country, footpaths or roads ran along the tops of dikes that were built alongside the canals. At crossing points along the Nile and its tributaries, small wooden ferries stood ready to escort travelers to the other side, for there were few bridges in the country. If no ferry or crossing planks were provided, then the traveler had no choice but to dive into the water and cross as quickly and quietly as possible, keeping a sharp eye out for hungry crocodiles and dangerous hippos.

Sometimes, travel was undertaken not for the entertainment of the rich but for spiritual reasons. In fact, the most common long-distance travelers in ancient Egypt were religious pilgrims on their way to a favored temple or shrine. Pierre Montet describes one such voyage to Abydos:

On these occasions travellers would embark on a vessel of archaic design, built up very high at the bow and stern—a sign that the voyage was strictly religious in character. Once on board they would take their seats in a cabin shaped like a shrine, as if they were in a summer-house in their own gardens, with food laid out on a tray in front of it. The forepart of the boat served as both slaughter-house and kitchen, and here an ox would be cut up and beer prepared so that the travellers could enjoy it fresh.[54]

For the ancient Egyptian, travel outside of his own homeland held little interest. Not only did travel itself present the threat of many dan-

gers and discomforts, but foreign lands were considered much less civilized than Egypt. The Egyptian man or woman also feared leaving behind the protection and guidance of the familiar gods of Egypt to travel in a place where the gods were unfamiliar and hostile.

Contact with the outside world was inevitable, however, and it was just such contact that brought about the end of Egypt's independence and ancient Egyptian society. In an attempt to merge her Ptolemaic dynasty with the most powerful rulers of Rome, Queen Cleopatra allied herself with the Roman leaders Julius Caesar and (after Caesar's assassination) Mark Antony. Cleopatra was the last of the Ptolemaic monarchs, outsiders descended from the Macedonian general Ptolemy, who was one of the leaders of Alexander the Great's army. Under the Ptolemaic rulers, who ruled from the new city of Alexandria, the Egyptians saw themselves losing status in their own country:

Native Egyptians [were] . . . expelled from Alexandria by royal decree, "with the exception of pig-dealers and river-boatmen and the men who bring down reeds for heating the baths." Outside the capital, they were second-class citizens in their own country, ruled in a foreign language, prevented from holding public office, burdened by heavy taxes and barred from owning property.[55]

Cleopatra and Mark Antony were defeated at the Battle of Actium in 31 B.C. by the Roman leader Octavius. The Egyptians then found themselves completely at the mercy of the most powerful state in the Mediterranean world. Roman ships soon appeared in Egyptian ports, their holds prepared for transporting Cleopatra's treasure and Egyptian grain back to storehouses in the Italian peninsula.

The alliance between Queen Cleopatra and Rome's Mark Antony, pictured here in an artist's rendering, marked the end of ancient Egypt's independence. Their forces were defeated by those of the Roman emperor Octavius at the Battle of Actium in 31 B.C.

Egypt became a mere province of Rome, occupied by Roman soldiers and governed by a Roman official. The Ptolemaic dynasty, along with the thirty-one dynasties of three millennia of Egyptian history, came to an end.

Gradually, under Roman control, the ancient traditions and culture of the Egyptians passed away. The state gods were forgotten, and the temples fell into disrepair. Artists copied the forms and scenes from the past, but many of their works turned out to be no more than lifeless imitations. The Egyptians forgot the time-honored funerary customs of the past, stopped building and preparing their elaborate tombs, and lost the art and science of mummification.

Work for the Egyptian farmer and artisan went on much as before, but the popular myths and beliefs that formed the underpinning of daily life slipped into the past. As a Roman province, Egypt kept its preeminent place as one of the world's most civilized and prosperous locales; the leaders of Rome even prohibited the Romans from moving there, fearing that the easy life in Egypt would soften and corrupt their own, supposedly more virtuous, people. But Rome's empire itself lasted only a few centuries, and after Rome's decline and fall, Egypt adopted an entirely new culture and religion brought by Islamic Arab invaders from the Middle East, bringing to an end an ancient way of life.

Notes

Chapter 1: Life and Work Along the Nile River

1. Quoted in Guillemette Andreu, *Egypt in the Age of the Pyramids*, trans. David Lorton. Ithaca, NY: Cornell University Press, 1997, p. 60.
2. Quoted in Andreu, *Egypt in the Age of the Pyramids*, pp. 106–107.
3. Quoted in Cyril Aldred, *The Egyptians*. New York: Thames and Hudson, 1998, p. 60.
4. Lionel Casson, *Ancient Egypt*. New York: Time Incorporated, 1965, p. 40.
5. Herodotus, *The Histories*, trans. Aubrey de Selincourt. New York: Penguin Books, 1954, p. 134.
6. James Henry Breasted, *A History of the Ancient Egyptians*. New York: Charles Scribner's Sons, 1908, p. 10.
7. Pierre Montet, *Everyday Life in Egypt in the Days of Ramesses the Great*. London: Edward Arnold, 1958, pp. 118–19.
8. Breasted, *A History of the Ancient Egyptians*, p. 85.
9. Barbara Mertz, *Red Land, Black Land: The World of the Ancient Egyptians*. New York: Coward-McCann, 1966, p. 75.
10. Quoted in Mertz, *Red Land, Black Land*, pp. 72–73.
11. Casson, *Ancient Egypt*, p. 14.

Chapter 2: The Pharaoh and His Court

12. Alan Gardiner, *Egypt of the Pharaohs*. London: Oxford University Press, 1961, pp. 59–60.
13. John A. Wilson, *The Culture of Ancient Egypt*. Chicago: University of Chicago Press, 1951, pp. 72–73.
14. Quoted in Lord Kinross, *Portrait of Egypt*. New York: William Morrow, 1966, p. 27.
15. Joyce Tyldesley, *Nefertiti: Egypt's Sun Queen*. New York: Viking, 1998, p. 30.
16. Quoted in Barry J. Kemp, *Ancient Egypt: Anatomy of a Civilization*. New York: Routledge, 1993, pp. 215–16.
17. Editors of Time-Life, *Egypt: Land of the Pharaohs*. Alexandria, VA: Time-Life Books, 1992, p. 144.
18. Charles Freeman, *The Legacy of Ancient Egypt*. New York: Facts On File, 1997, p. 75.
19. Wilson, *The Culture of Ancient Egypt*, pp. 172–73.
20. Quoted in Gardiner, *Egypt of the Pharaohs*, pp. 95–96.
21. Wilson, *The Culture of Ancient Egypt*, p. 186.
22. Quoted in Freeman, *The Legacy of Ancient Egypt*, p. 70.

Chapter 3: In the Service of the Pharaoh: Scribes, Doctors, Soldiers, and Slaves

23. Tyldesley, *Nefertiti*, p. 39.
24. Christine Hobson, *The World of the Pharaohs*. New York: Thames and Hudson, 1987, p. 162.
25. Freeman, *The Legacy of Ancient Egypt*, p. 116.
26. Quoted in T. G. H. James, *An Introduction to Ancient Egypt*. New York: Harper & Row, 1979, p. 108.

27. Casson, *Ancient Egypt*, pp. 97–98.

28. Quoted in Montet, *Everyday Life in Egypt*, p. 222.

29. Quoted in Kinross, *Portrait of Egypt*, p. 31.

30. Wilson, *The Culture of Ancient Egypt*, p. 187.

Chapter 4: Egyptian Art and Artisans

31. Quoted in Editors of Time-Life, *Egypt*, pp. 140–41.

32. Freeman, *The Legacy of Ancient Egypt*, p. 114.

33. Freeman, *The Legacy of Ancient Egypt*, p. 105.

34. George Hart, *Ancient Egypt*. Eyewitness Books. New York: Alfred A. Knopf, 1990, p. 42.

35. Mertz, *Red Land, Black Land*, p. 334.

36. John Romer, *Ancient Lives: Daily Life in the Egypt of the Pharaohs*. New York: Henry Holt, 1984, p. 20.

Chapter 5: A Lifetime Spent Preparing for Death

37. A. Rosalie David, *The Egyptian Kingdoms*. New York: Peter Bedrick Books, 1988, p. 81.

38. Editors of Time-Life, *Egypt*, p. 142.

39. Wilson, *The Culture of Ancient Egypt*, pp. 112–13.

40. Hobson, *The World of the Pharaohs*, p. 169.

41. Montet, *Everyday Life in Egypt*, p. 304.

42. Quoted in David P. Silverman, ed., *Ancient Egypt*. New York: Oxford University Press, 1997, p. 146.

43. Quoted in George Steindorff and Keith C. Seele, *When Egypt Ruled the East*. Chicago: University of Chicago Press, 1942, p. 139.

44. Breasted, *A History of the Ancient Egyptians*, pp. 59–60.

45. Editors of Time-Life, *Egypt*, p. 90.

46. Kinross, *Portrait of Egypt*, p. 28.

47. Mertz, *Red Land, Black Land*, p. 279.

Chapter 6: Leisure Time in Ancient Egypt

48. Herodotus, *The Histories*, pp. 152–53.

49. Montet, *Everyday Life in Egypt*, pp. 36–37.

50. "The Magic and Mysteries of Ancient Egypt." www.verdenet.com/isis.

51. Breasted, *A History of the Ancient Egyptians*, p. 32.

52. Andreu, *Egypt in the Age of the Pyramids*, p. 83.

53. Wilson, *The Culture of Ancient Egypt*, pp. 26–27.

54. Montet, *Everyday Life in Egypt*, p. 172.

55. Freeman, *The Legacy of Ancient Egypt*, p. 133.

Glossary

akhet: The first season of the year and the season of the Nile flood, which began in early summer and continued for two or three months.

Amon: A local god of Thebes who was shown in human form and also as a ram. Amon became a national deity during the New Kingdom, when his cult priesthood at Thebes rivaled the power and wealth of Egypt's kings.

Anubis: The jackal-headed god who presided over the rites of mummification.

Aten: The name given to the divinity worshiped by King Akhenaton, represented by the disk of the sun.

ba: The soul of the dead, shown as a bird with a human head, which wandered freely in the afterlife.

Bedouin: Nomadic desert dwellers who harried the Nile valley from their home in the Libyan Desert, to the west, and the Arabian Desert, to the east.

Bes: A household god depicted as a squat, ugly dwarf and considered the protector of the home and family.

canopic jars: Jars used to hold the essential organs of the dead after mummification.

clepsydra: Water clocks used to count the hours in ancient Egypt.

decan: The Egyptian week, consisting of ten days.

Delta: The region of Lower (northern) Egypt where, in ancient times, the Nile branched out into seven main channels.

Hathor: The goddess of music, dance, and love, who was shown with a human face and the ears or horns of cattle.

hieratic: A system of cursive writing developed from hieroglyphic picture symbols.

Horus: The son of Osiris and Isis, reputed to be the first king of Egypt. He was depicted in Egyptian art with the head of a falcon and wearing the "double crown" of Upper and Lower Egypt.

Isis: Sister and wife of Osiris, the king of the underworld. She was a powerful and popular symbol of fertility and a protector of women and children whose worship outlasted ancient Egypt itself in the Mediterranean world.

ka: In Egyptian religion, a person's spiritual double, which served as his or her soul after death.

mastaba: A rectangular structure built to shelter an underground tomb.

natron: A mineral salt mined in the desert and used to dry out bodies before mummification.

Nilometers: Gauges used to measure the annual flood of the Nile River.

nome: An ancient Egyptian province, presided over by a nomarch.

Nubians: People dwelling to the south of ancient Egypt, in what is now Sudan.

Osiris: Chief god of the underworld; he was killed by his evil brother Seth and was reborn. To the Egyptians, the myth of Osiris represented the annual flooding or "rebirth" of the Nile River.

ostraka: Small pottery shards used for everyday writing and as a practice-writing medium in ancient Egyptian schools.

peret: The second season of the year, when the inundated land of the Nile valley emerged after the annual flood.

Ptah: The god of artisans, who began as a local god in the Old Kingdom capital of Memphis. He was depicted in Egyptian art in human form, holding a staff.

Re: The sun god of Heliopolis who was raised to the status of a national deity during the Fifth Dynasty of the Old Kingdom.

sebakh: Crumbled mud brick taken from old homes and used as a fertilizer by Egyptian farmers.

senet: A popular board game played on a rectangular surface divided into thirty squares, on which opponents moved pebbles or small pieces of stone.

Seth: The evil brother of Osiris who reigned over Upper Egypt; the god of natural terrors such as dust storms, locust plagues, and the trackless desert.

shaduf: Devices used to raise water from natural rivers and artificial irrigation canals to the fields.

shemu: The third season of the year, the season of drought when the Nile River ran low and annual crops were harvested.

sistrum: A ceremonial rattle used at dancing or religious festivals.

Sobek: The crocodile god whose center of worship was at the town of Crocodilopolis. A ceremonial pool at this town was filled with sacred crocodiles, adorned with jewels.

sopdit: The Egyptian New Year, celebrated with the rising of Sirius in early summer.

Taweret: The god of pregnancy, birth, and childhood, represented by a pregnant hippo.

Thoth: The god of wisdom and knowledge who served as the scribe of the gods.

ushabti: Small statuettes that were placed in Egyptian tombs, intended to serve as replacements for the dead in the work they might be called on to perform in the afterlife.

vizier: The highest public official after the king, responsible for all aspects of the Egyptian administration.

For Further Reading

Marilyn Bridges, *Egypt: Antiquities from Above.* Boston: Little, Brown, 1996. A book of striking black-and-white aerial photographs, which illustrate the monuments of Egypt from the Old Kingdom to the Islamic period among their modern surroundings.

A. R. David and E. Tapp, *The Mummy's Tale: The Scientific and Medical Investigation of Natsef-Amun, Priest in the Temple at Karnak.* New York: St. Martin's Press, 1993. A medical examination team describes the use of radiology, CT scans, dental studies, and other modern methods in the investigation of the death and life of a three-thousand-year-old mummified priest.

Editors of Time-Life, *Egypt: Land of the Pharaohs.* Alexandria, VA: Time-Life Books, 1992. A popular, magazine-style history of ancient Egypt highlighting archaeological discoveries that cast light on the lives of Egypt's kings and royal families.

Barbara Ford and Howard Carter, *Searching for King Tut.* New York: W. H. Freeman, 1995. The life and digs of archaeologist Howard Carter, who discovered the tomb of King Tutankhamen in 1922.

Charles Freeman, *The Legacy of Ancient Egypt.* New York: Facts On File, 1997. A beautifully designed and illustrated book that gives updated details and discoveries on all aspects of life in ancient Egypt.

George Hart, *Ancient Egypt.* Eyewitness Books. New York: Alfred A. Knopf, 1990. A visual journey through everyday life in Egypt, giving a straightforward yet very detailed explanation of how the ancient Egyptians lived, worked, played, and fought their battles.

Nancy Jenkins, *The Boat Beneath the Pyramid.* London: Thames and Hudson, 1980. The excavation and reconstruction—out of 1,223 ancient wooden fragments—of a royal funerary barge, found near the Great Pyramid of Cheops.

Nicholas Reeves with Nan Froman, *Into the Mummy's Tomb.* Toronto, Ontario: Madison Press Books, 1992. Contemporary and historical photographs illustrate the discovery of King Tut's tomb and the artifacts found within.

Kent R. Weeks, *The Lost Tomb.* New York: William Morrow, 1998. Weeks describes his discovery of KV 5, the long-lost tomb of the sons of Ramses II, in the Valley of the Kings. This tomb proved to be the largest and most complicated mausoleum yet found.

Works Consulted

Books

Cyril Aldred, *The Egyptians*. New York: Thames and Hudson, 1998. A revised and updated edition of a scholarly work first published in 1961, in which the author painstakingly compiles literary and archaeological evidence to re-create a history of ancient Egypt from the Archaic (predynastic) period to the New Kingdom.

Guillemette Andreu, *Egypt in the Age of the Pyramids*. Trans. David Lorton. Ithaca, NY: Cornell University Press, 1997. A well-written, informative, and up-to-date discussion of Old Kingdom Egypt, written by a professor of hieroglyphics and Egyptologist at the Louvre museum of Paris.

James Henry Breasted, *A History of the Ancient Egyptians*. New York: Charles Scribner's Sons, 1908. A long, authoritative, and florid history of Egypt. Though some of the material is now dated thanks to twentieth-century archaeological discoveries, the book is still worth reading.

Lionel Casson, *Ancient Egypt*. New York: Time Incorporated, 1965. This edition from the Great Ages of Man series is a well-illustrated, but outdated, survey of Egyptian history, art, and society written by an authority on ancient civilizations.

A. Rosalie David, *The Egyptian Kingdoms*. New York: Peter Bedrick Books, 1988. A description of Egyptian society and history, including a chapter on modern explorers and archaeologists, a discussion of Egyptian religion, and sections on ancient Egyptian architecture and society; illustrated throughout with color photographs, artists' renderings of the sites in ancient times, and maps.

Charles Freeman, *The Legacy of Ancient Egypt*. New York: Facts On File, 1997. A comprehensive and lavishly illustrated book that gives the most recent discoveries of ancient Egypt in great detail. Contains many interesting sidebars and excellent maps.

Alan Gardiner, *Egypt of the Pharaohs*. London: Oxford University Press, 1961. A classic and well-written scholarly study of ancient Egypt, from prehistoric times to the last years of the New Kingdom, illustrated with fine, detailed photographs.

S. R. K. Glanville, ed., *The Legacy of Egypt*. Westport, CT: Greenwood Press, 1976. A collection of fifteen essays on Egyptian history and culture by leading experts in the field of Egyptology.

Herodotus, *The Histories*. Trans. Aubrey de Selincourt. New York: Penguin Books, 1954. The account of the Greek historian and traveler Herodotus, who visited Egypt in the fifth century B.C. and wrote a fascinating account of Egyptian farming, religion, society, and history as told to him by the Egyptians themselves.

Christine Hobson, *The World of the Pharaohs*. New York: Thames and Hudson, 1987. A book on Egyptian history and archaeology divided into short chapters giving the most recent discoveries in the ever-changing field of Egyptology.

T. G. H. James, *An Introduction to Ancient Egypt*. New York: Harper & Row, 1979. A survey of Egyptian language, literature, religion, art, and history, supplemented by interesting chapters on Roman and Coptic (Christian) Egypt.

Barry J. Kemp, *Ancient Egypt: Anatomy of a Civilization*. New York: Routledge, 1993. The author, a director of excavations at Akhenaten's city of el-Amarna, reconstructs ancient Egyptian society and mythology by examining recent archaeological evidence.

Lord Kinross, *Portrait of Egypt*. New York: William Morrow, 1966. A personal and anecdotal journey through Egypt, by a former first secretary of the British embassy and a skilled travel writer.

Barbara Mertz, *Red Land, Black Land: The World of the Ancient Egyptians*. New York: Coward-McCann, 1966. A conversational and very personal book on ancient Egyptian society, packed with information and including anecdotes on travel and archaeology in modern Egypt.

———, *Temples, Tombs and Hieroglyphs: A Popular History of Ancient Egypt*. New York: Peter Bedrick Books, 1990. A lively guide through Egypt for new students of the subject, emphasizing the role of art and religion in everyday life, and in which the author enjoys speculating on contentious and unresolved issues in ancient Egyptian history.

Pierre Montet, *Everyday Life in Egypt in the Days of Ramesses the Great*. London: Edward Arnold, 1958. A book on everyday life as described in archaeological finds, including papyri, wall paintings, and tombs from the New Kingdom reign of Ramses II; also contains descriptions of country and city homes, the arts and professions, travel, the army, burial rites, religion, and the family.

Michael Rice, *Egypt's Making: The Origins of Ancient Egypt 5000–2000 B.C.* London: Routledge, 1990. A book on the predynastic cultures of Egypt and their contribution to Egypt's Old Kingdom culture and government.

John Romer, *Ancient Lives: Daily Life in the Egypt of the Pharaohs*. New York: Henry Holt, 1984. An account of life in a Theban village inhabited by the masons, painters, scribes, foremen, and others who created the royal tombs of the Valley of the Kings.

David P. Silverman, ed., *Ancient Egypt*. New York: Oxford University Press, 1997. A series of articles written by various experts on aspects of ancient Egyptian civilization, including religious ritual, pyramid building, art, the status of women, and the history of Egypt's kingdoms and dynasties.

George Steindorff and Keith C. Seele, *When Egypt Ruled the East*. Chicago: University of Chicago Press, 1942. A well-illustrated scholarly history emphasizing the deeds and the legends of the Egyptian kings. Lengthy chapters on art, religion, and Akhenaton.

B. G. Trigger, B. J. Kemp, D. O'Connor, and A. B. Lloyd, *Ancient Egypt: A Social History*. Cambridge, England: Cambridge University Press, 1983. A series of scholarly articles on Egyptian prehistory and the three major periods of ancient Egyptian civilization, geared to the professor or university student of Egyptology.

Joyce Tyldesley, *Nefertiti: Egypt's Sun Queen*. New York: Viking, 1998. A book on Nefertiti, the queen of Akhenaton, and life in Akhenaton's royal capital at Tell el-Amarna. Although the subject of Akhenaton and his religious revolution has stirred a long and fascinating debate among historians, *Nefertiti* bogs down in details and speculation over the inconclusive evidence surrounding Akhenaton and the other members of his family and dynasty.

Dietrich Wildung, *Egypt: From Prehistory to the Romans*. Koln, Germany: Taschen, 1997. This volume from Taschen's World Architecture series is a beautifully illustrated book on Egyptian religious and secular architecture, offering detailed photographs, schematic drawings, and maps.

John A. Wilson, *The Culture of Ancient Egypt*. Chicago: University of Chicago Press, 1951. A book that explores the basic concepts and values underlying Egyptian society, and their effect on the course of ancient Egyptian history.

Internet Sources

Egyptian Tourism Ministry. http://interoz.com/egypt/bod9.htm.

"Internet Ancient History Sourcebook." www.fordham.edu/halsall/ancient/asbook1.html.

"The Magic and Mysteries of Ancient Egypt." www.verdenet.com/isis.

"The Page of Egyptian Medicine." www.teleport.com/~spindel/Egypt/EgyptPAge.html.

Index

women's quarters in, 52
Horus (god), 43, 73
hunting, 71–72
Hyksos, 10, 72

Imhotep, 50
infidelity, 21
"Internet Ancient History
    Sourcebook" (website),
    43
Isis (goddess), 70

jewelers, 48, 49
jewelry, 69
Julius Caesar, 76
justice, administration of,
    31

Kadesh, Battle of, 42
Kamose, 10
Karnak, 62, 64–66
Kheruef, 28–29
Khnum (god), 61, 62
Kingdoms
    Middle
        dance and, 70
        described, 8–10
        development of army
            during, 27
        peasants during, 32
        religion and, 56
    New
        establishment of, 10
        iron weapons and, 49
        music during, 71
        navy during, 42–43
        religion during, 62, 64

Old
    described, 8
    power of pharaohs
        during, 24
    pyramids of, 50, 53, 56
Kinross, Lord, 64

*Legacy of Ancient Egypt,
    The* (Freeman), 30–31
listeners, 43–44
literacy, 35, 36
litters, 75
Lower Egypt, 8

Mark Antony, 76
marriage, 21–22
mastabas, 50, 53, 56
medicine, 38–40
Megiddo, Battle of, 43
Memphis, 8, 22
Menes (pharaoh), 8
Mentuhotep I (pharaoh),
    8–9
Mertz, Barbara
    on festivals, 66
    on punishment for infi-
        delity, 21
    on tombs of pharaohs of
        Eighteenth Dynasty,
        51
metalsmiths, 48
monotheism, 63
Montet, Pierre
    on birthday of Set, 67–68
    on pilgrimages, 76
    on threshing grain, 17
Montu (god), 43

mortuary temples, 11,
    64–65
mummies, 29–30, 58–60
music, 70–71
myths, 26

navy, 42–43
Nefertiti (Tyldesley), 36
Nile River
    clay of, 49
    course of, 22
    Delta, 12
    flooding of
        agriculture and, 12–13
        calendar and, 16
        festivals and, 66, 67
        government projects
            and, 15
        pyramids and, 50
        religion and, 12
        importance of, 13
    nobles
        artisans and, 46, 51
        daily life of, 33
        in government, 30–32,
            33
        homes of, 19–20, 33–34
        hunting and, 71–72
        tomb robbing and, 44
        work of, 17
    nomarchs, 32
    Nun, 55

Octavius, 76
"Opening of the Mouth,
    the," 59
Osiris (god), 56, 62, 70

Thebes, 9, 10, 62, 64
Thoth (god), 62
timekeeping, 16
tombs, 51, 57
    importance of, 29
    mastabas, 50, 53, 56
    mortuary temples, 11,
        64–65
    theft and, 44
    see also pyramids
tools
    agricultural, 14, 15–16,
        17
    of artisans, 47
trade, 10, 43
travel, 75–76
Tutankhamen (pharaoh),
    63

Tyldesley, Joyce
    on foreign children in
        Egyptian schools, 36
    on *sed*, 28

Upper Egypt, 8

viziers, 31

weapons, 41–42, 49
Wilson, John A.
    on administration of jus-
        tice, 31
    on afterlife beliefs, 57
    on divinity of pharaohs,
        24–25
    on games and wealth, 74

on separation of classes,
    32
on slaves, 44
women
    agriculture and, 14, 16,
        17
    legal rights of, 20
    quarters for, 52
    as slaves, 44
    status of, 20
    work outside the home
        permitted, 20–21
*World of the Pharaohs,
    The* (Hobson), 26, 37
writing, 35, 38

Picture Credits

Cover photo: © Bojan Brecelj/Corbis
Alinari/Art Resource, NY, 29
Archive Photos, 47
© Joseph Beck, 1993/FPG International, 52
© Bojan Brecelj/Corbis, 15, 18, 21, 27, 30
Foto Marburg/Art Resource, NY, 68
FPG International, 49
© Lloyd Harvey, 1997/FPG International, 53
Hirz/Archive Photos, 74
© Charles & Josette Lenars/Corbis, 19

Eric Lessing/Art Resource, NY, 14, 20, 44, 50, 70, 73
© Ludovic Maisant/Corbis, 61
© Michael Nicholson/Corbis, 65
North Wind Picture Archives, 28, 75
© Gianni Dagli Orti/Corbis, 9, 23, 34, 36 (left and right), 40, 46, 57, 69
Scala/Art Resource, NY, 32, 38
Stock Montage, Inc., 16, 42, 60, 77
© Roger Wood/Corbis, 56, 63

About the Author

Thomas Streissguth was born in Washington, D.C., and grew up in Minnesota. After earning a B.A. in music, he traveled in Europe and worked as a teacher and book editor. He has written more than thirty books of nonfiction, including histories, biographies, and geographies, for children and young adults.